MW01267717

Why the Tool?

Tools have been important to the success of the human race since the dawn of time. Unlike other species, humans are adept at building and using tools to accomplish specific and important tasks. In the modern era, software tools are the latest innovation in moving humanity forward in the tools frontier. Microsoft is proud to continue to innovate and provide new software tools and contribute to an improved society for all.

The Needle-Nose Pliers

Pliers are hand-held tools for holding and gripping small objects or for bending and cutting small articles such as wire. The first usage of pliers can be traced back to the mid-sixteenth century. The word plier comes from the French word pli, which means to fold or twist together.

MICROSOFT®
VISUAL
STUDIO.NET

Based on Beta Content

Microsoft®

PUBLISHED BY
Microsoft Press
A Division of Microsoft Corporation
One Microsoft Way
Redmond, Washington 98052-6399

Library of Congress Cataloging-in-Publication Data
Microsoft Visual Studio .NET / Microsoft Corporation.
      p. cm.
    Includes index.
    ISBN 0-7356-1446-6
    1. Microsoft Visual studio.   2. Microsoft.net framework.   3. Web site
development--Computer programs.   4. Application software--Development--Computer
programs.   I. Microsoft Corporation.

TK5105.8885.M57 M53   2001
005.2'76--dc21   2001030472

Printed and bound in the United States of America.

1 2 3 4 5 6 7 8 9   QWE   6 5 4 3 2 1

Distributed in Canada by Penguin Books Canada Limited.

A CIP catalogue record for this book is available from the British Library.

Microsoft Press books are available through booksellers and distributors worldwide. For further information about international editions, contact your local Microsoft Corporation office or contact Microsoft Press International directly at fax (425) 936-7329. Visit our Web site at mspress.microsoft.com. Send comments to mspinput@microsoft.com.

Acquisitions Editor: Juliana Aldous
Project Editor: Denise Bankaitis

Body Part No. X08-19537

Contents

Preface..**vii**

Who Is This Book For? vii

What's in This Book? vii

A Warning... viii

About MSDN... viii

    MSDN Online.. viii

    MSDN Publications ix

    MSDN Subscriptions ix

Visual Studio.NET: Build Web Applications Faster and Easier
Using Web Services and XML **1**

Web Services and the Microsoft .NET Framework 2

A Web Services Example 3

New Features of the Visual Studio.NET IDE..6

New Features in Visual Basic.NET 8

New Features in C++ 10

A New Language: C# 10

New Features for Enterprise Development 11

Web Forms 12

Managing Web Application Data with ADO+..12

RAD for the Server 16

Lifecycle Tools..18

Conclusion...19

Unified IDE Maximizes Developer Productivity.....................................**21**

Shared Integrated Development Environment 21

    Start Page..22

    Solution Explorer 23

    Enhanced Toolbox 24

    Server Explorer 24

    Task List 25

    Dynamic Help 26

    Document Windows 26

    Command Window 28

Unified IDE Maximizes Developer Productivity *(continued)*

Window Management 28
    Auto Hide 28
    Dockable Windows 28
    Tabbed Documents..29
    IDE Navigation 29
    Favorites 29
    Multimonitor Support 29
Designers 29
    Web Form Designer 29
    Windows Forms Designer 29
    Component Designer 30
    XML Designer 30
Visual Studio Macros 30
Visual Database Tools 31
    Database Designer 31
    Query Designer 31
    Database Project 32
    Script Editor...32
    Stored Procedure Debugging 32
Conclusion 32

Preparing Your Visual Basic 6.0 Applications for the Upgrade to Visual Basic.NET 33
Overview 33
What Is Visual Basic.NET? 34
Why Is Visual Basic.NET Not 100% Compatible? 34
Upgrading to Visual Basic.NET...35
Working with Both Visual Basic 6.0 and Visual Basic.NET 37
Architecture Recommendations..37
    Browser-based Applications 38
    Client/Server Projects 39
    Single-tier Applications 39
    Data...40
Upgrading..41
    Variant to Object 41
    Integer to Short 41
    Property Syntax..41
    Visual Basic Forms to Windows Forms 42
    Interfaces 43

Upgrade Report and Comments 43
Programming Recommendations..44
    Use Early-Binding...44
    Use Date for Storing Dates 45
    Resolve Parameterless Default Properties 46
    Use Boolean Comparisons with AND/OR/NOT 47
    Avoid Null Propagation...50
    Use Zero Bound Arrays..51
    Use Constants Instead of Underlying Values..........................52
    Arrays and Fixed-Length Strings in User-Defined Types........52
    Avoid Legacy Features..53
    Windows APIs 54
    Considerations for Forms and Controls 57

Visual Basic for the Microsoft .NET Framework................................**59**
The Role of the CLR..60
Managed Types...61
Using the Visual Basic.NET Compiler 62
Delegates and Events 66
Microsoft Intermediate Language and JIT Compilation................69
The CLR as a Better COM 70
A Richer Format for Component Metadata 73
Garbage Collection for Managing Object Lifetimes......................75
Assemblies and Code Distribution 76
The End of DLL Hell 78
Visual Basic 6.0 to Visual Basic.NET Migration 79
Conclusion..80

C# Introduction and Overview..**81**
Microsoft Introduces C# 82
Productivity and Safety..82
    Embraces emerging Web programming standards....................82
    Eliminates costly programming errors 83
    Reduces ongoing development costs with built-in support for versioning 83
Power, Expressiveness, and Flexibility 84
    Better mapping between business process and implementation..............................84
    Extensive interoperability 84
Conclusion..85

Sharp New Language: C# Offers the Power of C++ and Simplicity of Visual Basic 87

Simplicity 88

Consistency.. 89

Modernity 92

Object Oriented.. 93

Type Safety 94

Scalability 97

Version Support 97

Compatibility.. 98

Flexibility 100

Availability 100

Programming in C#: Technobabble 101

C#: A Message Queuing Application 113

Introduction 113

The .NET Framework Application 114

    Application Structure.. 114

    Service Classes 116

    Instrumentation 126

    Installation 128

Conclusion 129

Introducing JScript.NET 131

What About VBScript? 131

JScript.NET 132

    Evolution 133

    Working closely with ECMA 133

    Performance... 133

    Compilation 138

    Productivity... 138

    Examples Using JScript.NET 143

Summary 147

Preface

If you are holding this book in your hands, no doubt you want information about Microsoft .NET and you want it now. You have heard about how .NET will allow developers to create programs that will transcend device boundaries and fully harness the connectivity of the Internet in their applications. You have read in the news journals that Microsoft will soon be releasing a new programming language called C# that is derived from C and C++ and is part of Visual Studio.NET. You are curious about .NET, what Microsoft has planned, and how you can be a part of it.

This book contains some of the most requested topics on Microsoft .NET available through the Microsoft Developer Network (MSDN)—Microsoft's premier developer resource. *Microsoft Visual Studio.NET* is one book in a series that includes *The Microsoft .NET Framework, The Microsoft .NET Framework Developer Specifications, Web Applications in the Microsoft .NET Framework*, and *Microsoft C# Language Specifications*. Within this series, you'll find important technical articles from *MSDN Magazine* and MSDN Online as well as subject matter overviews and white papers from Microsoft and industry experts. You will also find transcripts of key speeches and interviews with top Microsoft product managers. We have also included the documentation and specifications for the new C# language and other key documents. And code…lots and lots of code.

Who Is This Book For?

This book is for developers who are interested in being on the cutting edge of new technologies and languages. It's for developers who are eager to learn, want to stay ahead of the curve, and aren't willing to wait until everything is in place and wrapped up in a pretty package. If you fit these criteria, order a pizza and settle in—this book is for you.

What's in This Book?

This book focuses on Visual Studio.NET—the complete tool for rapidly building .NET enterprise applications that enable developers to build solutions in the language of their choice, such as Visual Basic.NET, Visual C++, or the newest language, C#. Starting with a broad overview of the new features of Visual Studio.NET, the book then zooms in and provides more information on the different languages. Whether you're currently programming with Visual Basic, C++, or eager to start working with C#, you'll gain an understanding of the benefits and how to prepare for Visual Studio.NET.

The first article includes an overview of the key features of Visual Studio.NET including a Shared Integrated Development Environment (IDE), windows management, Web Form and Window Form Designers, Visual Studio macros, and Visual Database Tools. If you are a Visual Basic programmer, you will especially want to take a look at the next two articles. The first, from MSDN Online, describes how to prepare Visual Basic 6.0 Applications for the upgrade to Visual Basic.NET. Next up is an in-depth article explaining the new features of Visual Studio.NET by Ted Pattison of DevelopMentor.

The next set of articles all focus on the new object-oriented language called C#. Included is a general introduction and overview of C#, which is followed by MSDN Magazine's own Joshua Trupin's article on C#—outlining the differences you'll find between C# and Visual Basic and C++. Next Carl Nolan of the Microsoft E-Commerce Solutions Team demonstrates a Windows Service solution using C# and the .NET Framework. Finally, Andrew Clinick, a program manager in the Microsoft Script Technology Group, introduces JScript.NET.

Of course, while reading is useful, there is nothing quite like working directly with Visual Studio.NET itself. We encourage you to visit MSDN online and download the current Visual Studio.NET beta and take it for a test drive.

A Warning

Microsoft is offering this material as a first look, but remember that it's not final. Be sure to read any warnings posted on MSDN before installing any beta products. Visit MSDN regularly, and check for updates and the latest information.

About MSDN

MSDN makes it easy to find timely, comprehensive development resources and stay current on development trends and Microsoft technology. MSDN helps you keep in touch with the development community, giving you opportunities to share information and ideas with your peers and communicate directly with Microsoft. Check out the many resources of MSDN.

MSDN Online

More than just technical articles and documentation, MSDN Online (http://msdn.microsoft.com) is the place to go when looking for Microsoft developer resources. On MSDN Online, you can

- Search the MSDN Library and Knowledge Base for technical documentation
- Visit an online Developer Center for resource listings on popular topics
- View and download sample applications and code, or make and review comments through the Code Center

- Participate in peer developer forums such as Newsgroups, Peer Journal, Members Helping Members, and Ratings & Comments
- Find technical seminars, trade shows, and conferences sponsored or supported by Microsoft, and then easily register online

MSDN Publications

MSDN Publications (http://msdn.microsoft.com/magazines) offers print and online publications for current information on all types of development. The following is a list of just a few of the publications MSDN produces.

- *MSDN Magazine*—a monthly magazine featuring real-world solutions built with Microsoft technologies, as well as early looks at upcoming products and new directions, such as Microsoft .NET
- *The .NET Show* (MSDN Show)—a regular series of webcasts about Microsoft's hottest technologies
- *MSDN Online Voices*—an online collection of regular technical columns updated each week
- *MSDN News*—a bimonthly newspaper of technical articles and columns for MSDN subscribers

MSDN Subscriptions

With an MSDN subscription (http://msdn.microsoft.com/subscriptions), you can get your hands on essential Microsoft developer tools, Microsoft .NET Servers, Visual Studio.NET, and Microsoft operating systems. Available on CD and DVD, as well as online through MSDN Subscriber downloads, an MSDN subscription also provides you with

- Monthly shipments of the latest Microsoft Visual Studio development system, Microsoft .NET Enterprise Servers, Microsoft operating systems, and Visio 2000
- The latest updates, SDKs, DDKs, and essential programming information

Visual Studio.NET:
Build Web Applications Faster
and Easier Using Web Services
and XML

This article by Dave Mendlen, product planner for Visual Basic, was published in MSDN Magazine *in September 2000. Visual Studio.NET incorporates exciting features, some of which are improvements on previous versions and some of which are brand-new. Some of the key additions are the new Microsoft programming language called C#, a new and smarter integrated development environment, new object-oriented features in Visual Basic.NET, and development life cycle tools. This article provides an overview of these features as well as a look at Web Services, Web Forms, and new versions of ActiveX Data Objects and Active Server Pages.*

The upcoming release of Visual Studio®.NET provides a rich set of features and productivity tools that allow developers to rapidly create enterprise-scale applications for the Web Services Platform. In this article I'll cover the Web Services Platform and what you can expect to see in this Visual Studio release for quickly creating, deploying, and maintaining Web Services. I'll describe the new features of the integrated development environment, Visual Basic®, C++, and a new language, C# (pronounced "C sharp"). I'll also give you a brief look at Web Forms and how Active Server Pages+ (ASP+) eases Web Form implementation, ActiveX Data Objects+ (ADO+) and how datasets make data available for your Web applications, new tools and templates for enterprise development, enhanced support for XML, new features supporting RAD on the server, and the latest tools in Visual Studio that support the development life cycle. Figure 1 illustrates the relationship between the topics I'll cover. As with all product previews, details are subject to change before the product ships, but the information in the article should help you start thinking about how to take advantage of all these great new features.

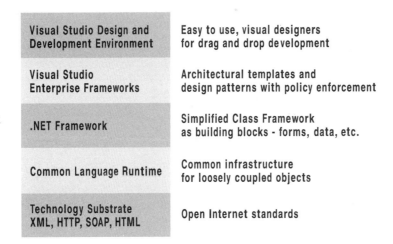

Visual Studio Design and Development Environment	Easy to use, visual designers for drag and drop development
Visual Studio Enterprise Frameworks	Architectural templates and design patterns with policy enforcement
.NET Framework	Simplified Class Framework as building blocks - forms, data, etc.
Common Language Runtime	Common infrastructure for loosely coupled objects
Technology Substrate XML, HTTP, SOAP, HTML	Open Internet standards

Figure 1. Visual Studio.NET Architecture

Web Services and the Microsoft .NET Framework

As the Web is evolving and technologies for universal data exchange such as XML are beginning to proliferate, a new development paradigm has emerged where software is seen as a collection of readily available Web Services that can be distributed and accessed via standard Internet protocols. Web Services provide middle-tier business functionality exposed via standard Web protocols. Since they use HTTP as a transport, they allow remote method requests to pass through enterprise firewalls. For security, both Secure Sockets Layer (SSL) and standard authentication techniques are supported. Using XML to invoke and return data from these Web Services means that programs written in any language, using any component model, and running on any operating system can access this functionality.

Obviously, the advantages of the model are many. Not only can companies more easily integrate internal applications, but they can also access services exposed by other businesses. By combining Web Services exposed on the Internet, companies can create a wide variety of value-added applications. For example, a company could unify banking, electronic bill payment, stock trading, and insurance services into a single, seamless financial management portal. Or they could integrate inventory control, fulfillment mechanisms, and purchase order tracking into a comprehensive supply chain management system.

While the Web Services model does not require any particular platform for hosting, being able to easily deploy and maintain a Web Service capable of supporting millions of clients requires the proper infrastructure. The Microsoft® .NET Framework has been designed to provide the tools and technologies necessary to support that infrastructure. In short, the framework is an extension of Windows® DNA 2000 with specific support for service delivery, service integration, and long running operations.

The heart of the Microsoft .NET Framework is a common language runtime that manages the needs of running code written in any Visual Studio programming language. This runtime supplies many services that help simplify code development and application deployment while also improving application reliability. The framework also supplies a set of class libraries that developers can use from any programming language. The framework provides specific support for building traditional Windows-based applications, Web applications, Web Services, and components. For more information on the Microsoft .NET Framework, read Mary Kirtland's article "The Programmable Web: Web Services Provides Building Blocks for the Microsoft .NET Framework," in this issue.

In Visual Studio.NET, you can easily expose any function—in any language—as a Web Service. There is no need to learn XML and SOAP to take advantage of Web Services. When you compile your business objects, Visual Studio.NET will automatically generate an XML file that describes the function, and when it is called the function will automatically send and receive XML packets.

After the Web Service has been built, both the compiled code and the XML file describing the public methods of the service are published to the Web server. The Web Service can now be invoked via HTTP, and XML will automatically be used to pass data to and from the service.

In Visual Studio.NET, you can drag any exposed Web Service directly into your application. Doing so enables Visual Studio to treat the Web Service as a class. Calling the Web Service is as simple as creating a new instance of the Web Service class and then calling its exposed methods.

A Web Services Example

Let's take a look at an example of how you can assemble an application from Web Services. This example uses Visual Basic, but the same tools for simplifying Web Service creation are available in other language products in Visual Studio. The Web Service in this example performs stock ratings.

First you would create a new Web Service project in Visual Basic called Stocks, as shown in Figure 2. Next, you would add a new class, called Ratings, to the project and write the code for the function to call the service, as shown in Figure 3.

Figure 2. Web Service Project in Visual Basic.NET

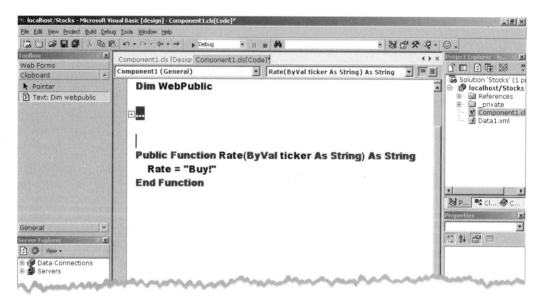

Figure 3. Adding a New Class to a Web Service Project

When you build the project, Visual Studio automatically creates an XML file that describes the Rate function, as follows:

```
<?xml version='1.0' ?>

<methods href='http://localhost/Stocks/Ratings'>
   <method name='Rate' href='Rate'>
      <request>
         <param dt='string'>ticker</param>
```

```
        </request>
        <response dt='string'/>
    </method>
</methods>
```

After the Web Service has been built, both the compiled code and the XML file describing the public methods of the service are published to the Web server. The Web Service can now be invoked via HTTP, and XML can be used to pass data to and from the service. You can test the Rate service directly from any type of browser that you'd like to use. As you can see in Figure 4, Visual Basic is passing data back natively as XML.

Figure 4. XML Output

To use a Web Service, all you need to do is drop the Web Service XML file into a project since it contains the URL of the Web Service as well as all the functions that are available. Visual Studio automatically creates the plumbing necessary to call the service.

Notice in Figure 5 that the stock rating service XML file has been included in the project. Visual Studio can now provide full statement completion when you access the Web Service. The stock rating service could also have been created on any operating system, including flavors of Unix, with any Web server, including Apache. However, using Microsoft Windows 2000 and Internet Information Services (IIS) 5.0 will make creating and assembling these services very easy and automatic.

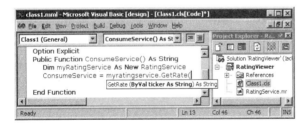

Figure 5. Stock Rating Service

New Features of the Visual Studio.NET IDE

Visual Studio.NET has a new, almost completely customizable shell that brings Visual Basic, Visual C++®, and Visual FoxPro® into a common integrated development environment (IDE). Because Web development deeply permeates Visual Studio.NET, the functionality originally found in Visual InterDev® is now a core part of the environment itself and is accessible from the various language products. Regardless of the language chosen for development, there is now just one environment to learn, configure, and use. You don't have to switch back and forth between environments to build, debug, and deploy your code. The net result is faster, easier development of enterprise applications. Whether you're building single language applications or creating mixed-language solutions, the common IDE supports high productivity development via drag and drop visual designers for HTML, XML, data, server-side code, and more.

In addition, the common IDE provides end-to-end debugging of Web applications across languages, projects, processes, and stored procedures. My favorite new features, which I'll describe later, include Dynamic Help, the Visual Web Page Editor, the Task List, the Object Browser, the new Command window functionality, Visual Basic for Applications (VBA) integration, Auto-Hide windows, multiple monitor support, and Office-style menus. Some of the new features are highlighted in Figure 6.

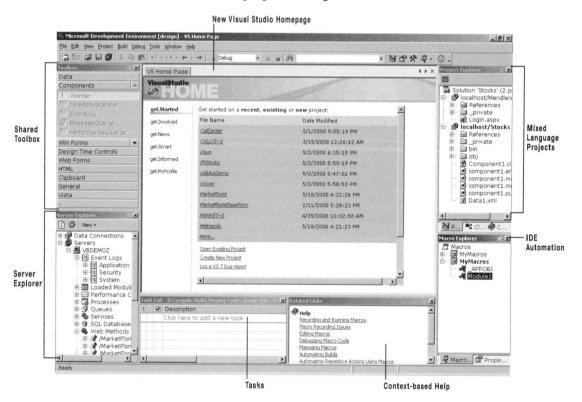

Figure 6. New Features in Visual Studio.NET

In order to find the right information at the right time from the MSDN® library, the Visual Studio IDE can now display links to related documentation (including *MSDN Magazine* articles!) based on the features or technologies currently in use. For example, you're in the IDE but don't have an application or component open, the environment displays links to information on how to plan an application, a selection of common business templates and wizards, and a dynamic list of application templates from various vendors. As you progress through the creation of your application, the IDE knows what part of the application you are working on and displays appropriate content in the Dynamic Help window.

The new Visual Web Page Editor is a shared WYSIWYG Web page editor that provides a graphical way to develop Web pages without delving into HTML or script code. The Web Page Editor provides a number of helpful facilities such as HTML tag and statement completion, design-time syntax-checking of XML, and absolute positioning of elements.

The Task List feature, formerly available only to developers working in Visual C++, now works across all Visual Studio-based languages and projects and allows developers to mark their code with comments related to tasks they need to do. These tasks are parsed and displayed in an easy tabular format in the Tasks window. This feature makes it easy for you to annotate your code so that when you or another member of your team opens it later, the exact state of the code can be understood with minimal pain. Double-clicking on the code comment in the Task List displays the section of code containing the comment.

An object browser is nothing new to programmers who use Visual Basic, but the new Object Browser for Visual Studio maps all objects on the system and provides detailed information about each. You can search for the information you need using the Object Browser's advanced filtering, sorting, and grouping features regardless of the language used to develop the object.

The Command Window allows you to more quickly harness the power of the IDE by providing a single input line to find, navigate, and execute the many possible elements within and outside the IDE. If you prefer the keyboard, you can utilize the Command Window as a method to perform searches, navigate to windows and items within a solution, execute commands, navigate the Web, and run external programs. The IDE's IntelliSense® feature has been extended to the Command Windowwhere it suggests a match based on entries you have typed previously.

The IDE is now completely customizable and extensible using VBA macrorecordingand programming. Almost the entire range of IDE sub-systems are available for customization and automation. The addition of VBA support simplifies the process of integrating other tools or applications (such as Microsoft Project or Outlook®) into the development cycle. On-the-fly customization and invocation of macros can be coded in the Command Window for an additional level of control.

With the move toward cross-language projects, Visual Studio.NET supports debugging across multiple languages contained in one solution. Using the debugger, developers can step seamlessly between HTML, script, and code—complete with integrated call stacks—offering a total solution for end-to-end development.

Another great new productivity feature in Visual Studio.NET is Auto-Hide windows. When you are finished using a window such as the toolbox, it simply collapses to the side of the screen. When you're ready to use it again, simply move your mouse over the collapsed window to expand it. This feature works with all of the shared windows so that you can have the maximum amount of screen real estate as you code. Another way to get additional real estate is by adding monitors; Visual Studio.NET now fully supports multiple monitor configurations.

Visual Studio also implements a feature you may have seen in Office 2000: menus that hide the least-used menu options. If you need to get to a hidden menu option, simply hold the mouse over the menu for one second to see the complete list of menu options. These settings are all user configurable so that you can turn off the productivity features that you don't need.

New Features in Visual Basic.NET

To rapidly build enterprise Web applications, developers must rely on business logic that is scalable, robust, and reusable. Over the past several years, object-oriented programming has emerged as the primary methodology for building systems that meet these requirements. Using object-oriented programming languages helps make large-scale systems easier to understand, simpler to debug, and faster to update.

While Visual Basic is a popular tool for rapid development of Windows-based applications, its lack of object-oriented language features sometimes limited its acceptance for creating middle-tier components. To address this issue, the upcoming release of Visual Basic has object-oriented language features to simplify the development of enterprise Web applications. With these new language features, Visual Basic delivers the power of C++ or the Java language while maintaining the instant accessibility that has made it such a popular development tool. I'll briefly describe new support in Visual Basic for inheritance, overloading, polymorphism, error handling with try...catch...finally, and freethreading. For a full treatment of new features in Visual Basic, see "The Future of Visual Basic: Web Forms, Web Services, and Language Enhancements Slated for Next Generation," by Joshua Trupin in the April 2000 issue of *MSDN Magazine* (http://msdn.microsoft.com/msdnmag/issues/0400/vbnexgen/vbnexgen.asp).

The most requested feature for Visual Basic has been support for implementation inheritance. In the upcoming release, Visual Basic has a new Inherits keyword to facilitate implementation inheritance as part of a class definition.

The new version of Visual Basic also supports overloading. Overloading allows an object's methods and operators to have different meanings depending on its context. Operators can behave differently depending on the data type, or class, of the operands. For example, *x+y* can mean different things depending on whether x and *y* are integers, strings, or structures. Overloading is especially useful when your object model dictates that you employ similar names for procedures that operate on different data types. A class that can display several different data types could have Display procedures that look like this:

```
Overloads Sub Display (theChar As Char)
...
Overloads Sub Display (theInteger As Integer)
...
Overloads Sub Display (theDouble As Double)
```

Without overloading, you'd have to create distinct names for each procedure (DisplayChar, DisplayInt, and DisplayDouble), even though they do the same thing.

Polymorphism refers to the ability of Visual Basic to process objects differently, depending on their data type or class. Additionally, it provides the ability to redefine methods for derived classes. For example, given a base class of Employee, polymorphism enables the programmer to define different PayEmployee methods for any number of derived classes, such as Hourly, Salaried, or Commissioned. No matter what type of an Employee an object is, applying the PayEmployee method to it will return the correct results, as shown in the following example:

```
Class Employee
   Function PayEmployee()
      PayEmployee = Hours * HourlyRate
   End Function

Class CommissionedEmployee
   Inherits Employee
   Overloads Function PayEmployee()
      PayEmployee = BasePay + Commissions
   End Function
```

In the past, error handling in Visual Basic meant providing error-handling code in every function and subroutine, resulting in scads of duplicate code. Error handling using the existing On Error GoTo statement sometimes slowed the development and maintenance of large applications. Its very name reflects some of these problems: As the GoTo implies, control is transferred to a labeled location inside the subroutine when an error occurs. Once the error code runs, it must often be diverted with another cleanup location via a standard GoTo, which uses yet another GoTo or an Exit out of the procedure. Handling several different errors with various combinations of Resume and Next quickly produces illegible code and leads to bugs when execution paths aren't completely thought out.

With the new try...catch...finally functionality of Visual Basic, these problems go away. Exception handling can be nested and there is a control structure for writing cleanup code that executes in both normal and exception conditions.

Visual Basic code today is synchronous, meaning that each line of code must be executed before the next one, but when developing Web applications, scalability is key and developers need tools that enable concurrent processing. The new version of Visual Basic implements freethreading. With the inclusion of freethreading, developers can spawn a thread (which can then perform some long-running task, execute a complex query, or run a complex calculation) while the rest of the application continues synchronously.

New Features in C++

Starting with Visual Studio.NET, the basic C++ language has been extended to provide support for programming to the new Microsoft .NET Framework. New to C++ are Managed Extensions, which are a set of upward compatible keywords and attributes that provide a familiar way to migrate an existing C++ application to the Microsoft .NET Framework. With a single compile, you can begin accessing the features of the framework without having to give up any of the traditional benefits of C++ that you have come to love, such as custom memory allocation, direct access to the Windows APIs, and efficient manipulation of low-level machine details.

Using data that conforms to the new Unified Type System makes any class you create in C++ immediately accessible in any other language in Visual Studio that targets the Microsoft .NET Framework. Inheritance across languages is finally possible.

Memory management has also been enhanced. Managed Extensions provide access to a garbage-collected memory heap and automatically manage objects allocated from this heap. Garbage collection means an automatic performance boost for most applications and allows the developer to focus on more important aspects of the application instead of the management of objects and pointers. Watch for more information about new C++ features in upcoming issues of *MSDN Magazine*.

A New Language: C#

C# is an elegant, simple, type-safe, object-oriented language designed to bring rapid application development (RAD) to the C and C++ developer without sacrificing the power and control that has been a hallmark of C/C++. Since Joshua Trupin's article, "Get Sharp this Summer: C# Offers Power of C++ and Simplicity of Visual Basic," in this issue provides details and examples, I'll just summarize a few of the key features of C#:

- A model and syntax that is familiar to C++ programmers because statement, expressions, and operators have 99 percent overlap with C++.
- Full interoperability with COM+ services.
- Full COM and platform support to make it easy to migrate your existing code.

- Automatic garbage collection.
- Type safety. There are no initialized variables and no unsafe casts. Array accesses are range-checked and operations and conversions are checked for overflow.
- Extensible and typed metadata, allowing the declaration of new types and categories of metadata.
- XML support for Web-based component interaction.

New Features for Enterprise Development

The new Visual Studio Enterprise Frameworks (VSEF) provide organizations with the ability to define project policies and best practices, then communicate them from within the Visual Studio IDE to enforce adherence to architectural and technologydecisions. There are two primary components to VSEF: Enterprise Templates and Policy Definition.

Enterprise Templates enable organizations to create standard templates for common solutions. A multitiered architecture such as Windows DNA 2000 can be captured at a high level as a solution containing specific project types at each of the logical application tiers. Microsoft provides a number of these templates with Visual Studio, including Windows DNA and Web Services templates. An additional benefit to developers and organizations is the extensibility of these templates. Templates are completely customizable using an XML schema to meet the specific needs of an organization.

The second primary feature delivered as part of VSEF is policy definition. Policy definition lets organizations filter the menu, dialog, and component choices available within the IDE. These policy definitions can be attached to architectural templates, allowing developers to more easily match specified business practices. For example, in the Windows DNA template, the business logic project should not contain any user interface components, so an architect might define a policy that says Web Forms and Win Forms cannot be used in that particular project. Architects can take this process even further and narrow the choices for specific technologies such as data access mechanism, default properties or settings, and appropriate ranges for properties. By narrowing the implementation details to appropriate technologies and choices, VSEF provides a more productive environment for developers and a higher likelihood of success in their application development projects.

The combination of Enterprise Templates and Policy Definition enables organizations to create a set of best practices and to communicate them with their developers in an efficient and effective manner. Customers can extend the VSEF features further by including links to custom topics and information that is viewable in the Dynamic Help window. For example, an organization may decide to standardize on ActiveX® Data Objects (ADO) as their data access methodology and enforce this decision through a policy definition that they can attach to an architecture template. The organization can include information that explains the policy and why it exists. When a developer is implementing data access code and has questions about what the policy is and why it exists, he will be able to select the link in the Dynamic Help window to view the corporate policy.

Web Forms

The next version of Visual Studio introduces a new technology called ASP+ Web Forms that simplifies the development of scalable Web applications. Modeled after forms in Visual Basic, Web Forms allow developers to rapidly develop cross-platform, cross-browser, programmable Web applications using the very same techniques already used in Visual Basic to build form-based desktop applications—drag controls to a form, double-click on a control, write some code, and press F5 to run the application.

A standard Web Forms page consists of an HTML file containing the visual representation of the page and a source file with event-handling code. The source is compiled into executable code, providing fast runtime performance. Both files resideand execute on the server where they generate an HTML 3.2-compliant document that's sent to the client.

The advantage of Web Forms over ASP pages and WebClasses is that Web Forms implement the full Visual Basic or C# language (or any compliant language) on the server. The code compiles and executes on the server for maximum performance and scalability. Additionally, Web Forms are more maintainable because they cleanly separate user interface (the HTML file) from code (a class file). Today, ASP code requires you to commingle HTML and script code on a page. With Web Forms, developers can write all the code while offloading the HTML file design to a graphic artist.

Web Forms also enable applications to run on any browser on any platform. You can build pages that are pure HTML 3.2 or you can specify a particular browser target.

Managing Web Application Data with ADO+

ADO+ is an improvement to ADO that provides platform interoperability and scalable data access. Because XML is the format for transmitting data, any application that can read the XML format can process data. In the most extreme case, the receiving component need not be an ADO+ component at all. It might be a Visual Studio-based solution or any application running on any platform. ADO+ was expressly built with these scenarios in mind.

Datasets are new to ADO+. A dataset is an in-memory copy of database data that contains any number of data tables, each of which typically corresponds to a database table or view. A dataset constitutes a disconnected view of the database data. That is, the data set exists in memory without an active connection to a database containing the corresponding tables or views to support the needs of Web applications.

At runtime, data will be passed from the database to a middle-tier business object and then down to the user interface. The data exchange uses an XML-based persistence and transmission format. To transmit data from one tier to another, an ADO+ solution expresses the in-memory data (the dataset) as an XML file and then sends the XML file to the other component. You can navigate and manipulate the data as an XML tree and use schema to view the XML data relationally. Figure 7 illustrates the major components of an ADO+ solution.

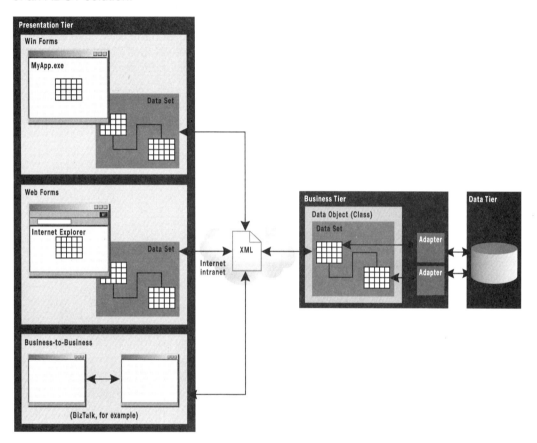

Figure 7. Major Components of an ADO+ Solution

In Visual Studio.NET, it is possible to program against your data objects, rather than against tables and columns. For example, consider the following line of code, using conventional (not strongly typed) programming:

```
IF TotalCost > Table("Customer").Column("AvailableCredit")
```

With the strongly typed programming of ADO+, the same example is much easier to write and read:

```
IF TotalCost > Customer.AvailableCredit
```

You'll also like how automatic statement completion is sensitive to the objects you are programming. Because the XML schema can be interpreted on the fly, IntelliSense is able to list the available tables related to Customers, as shown in Figure 8.

```
Private Sub Button1_Click(ByVal sender As System.Object
    Dim x As New Customers.
End Sub               | Orders |
```

Figure 8. IntelliSense Finds Order Table

There are a host of new features to make working with the XML data easy in Visual Studio.NET. For instance, for the hardcore XML developer there is a color-coded XML editor with statement and tag completion as shown in Figure 9.

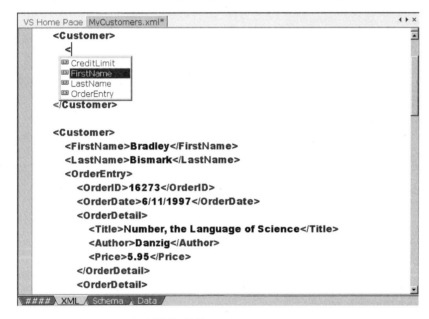

Figure 9. Color-coded XML Editor

You can also interact with a graphical view of data using the design view of the Dataset Designer, shown in Figure 10. Simply drag and drop tables from any data source, including SQL Server™ and Oracle databases, from the Server Explorer to the design surface. You can create datasets that are made up of data from any source, including relational databases, data entities created during design time, and even XML files.

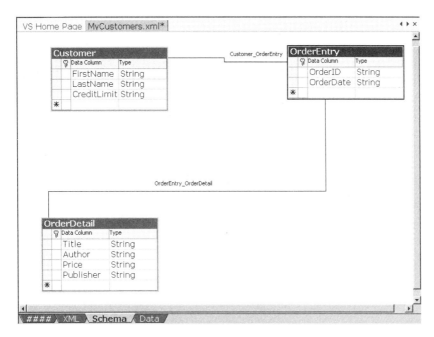

Figure 10. Dataset Designer

Often you need to add, modify, or delete data while you are designing your application. From the Data Preview tab, you can not only add and modify data, but also navigate the relationships of your data, as shown in Figure 11.

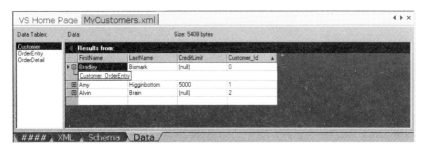

Figure 11. Data Preview

The data binding technologies for Visual Studio.NET have also been dramatically improved to take full advantage of ADO+, so building user interfaces that interact with data is easy. More importantly, you can now bind values to business objects and Web Services.

RAD for the Server

The key to building scalable Web applications is to focus on the middle tier. The business logic and the bulk of the application occur on middle-tier servers. The next version of the Visual Studio development system provides several new features including the Server Explorer and the Component Designer. They allow the same RAD using reusable server components that developers who use Visual Basic have used to rapidly assemble Windows-based user interfaces, applying this technique to the construction of middle-tier objects.

One of the biggest challenges in writing a middle-tier component is discovering what application services are available on the corporate network. And they can be very difficult to integrate into your application components.

If you have used Visual Studio 6.0, you know that discovery of Microsoft SQL Server and Oracle databases was enabled, and Visual Studio could manipulate the schema and data in those databases. Using the Data View window, you could point to a database and then expand nodes to drill down into the structure of the database and even modify the structure of the database or the tables, views, and stored procedures.

The next version of Server Explorer takes a giant step forward from the Visual Studio 6.0 Data View and shows the resources from an entire computer—including databases, message queues, and all other installed server elements that live there (see Figure 12).

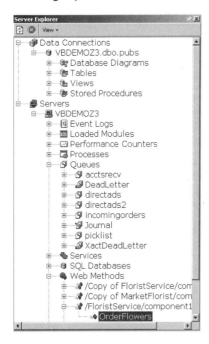

Figure 12. Server Explorer

You can also use Server Explorer to perform administrative tasks on your server resources. For example, you can add, delete, or rename a message queue, or start and stop a Windows NT® service from within the Visual Studio IDE.

Once you know what resources exist, you can drag these resources from Server Explorer to the designers in Visual Studio. In the same way that forms designers enable rapid creation of client applications, Server Explorer provides a way to build server-side components quickly and graphically. When you add one of these items to your designer, Visual Studio automatically creates a component that references the specific resource you selected.

For example, you might choose a specific message queue and drag and drop it to the design surface in the Component Designer. Visual Studio will automatically create a Message Queue component that references that specific queue, as shown in Figure 13. Just double-click the server component on the Component Designer, and the code for that object is opened.

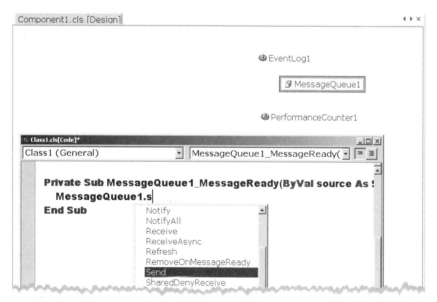

Figure 13. Message Queue

Lifecycle Tools

With Visual Studio.NET, Microsoft is focusing more broadly on the overall development life-cycle. Built with Internet scalability in mind along with an open and extensible architecture, Visual Studio.NET is the foundation for a lifecycle platform. As shown in Figure 14, Visual Studio addresses each of the phases in the development lifecycle as well as providing the key infrastructure for team management and collaboration.

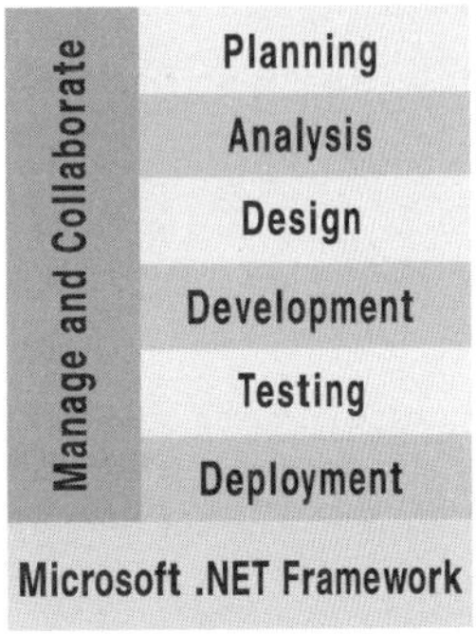

Figure 14. Dev Lifecycle

In Visual Studio.NET, Microsoft plans to deliver the key features and tools I've discussed here and is working closely with third parties to fill out the breadth of the lifecycle. This release will include features that address the analysis, design, testing, and deployment phases of the enterprise lifecycle.

To support the analysis and design phase, Visual Studio provides some significant enhancements to modeling tools. Information about these tools will be available at a later date. For the design and development phase, Visual Studio includes a full set of tools, as seen from the descriptions in this article. Both physical and logical design tools as well as a rich set of visual development tools are integrated into the IDE. As an example, a database developer can logically design his database, seamlessly convert it into a physical model, and then use the visual development tools to create stored procedures, views, user defined functions, and queries.

Visual Studio Web Test is fully integrated in the Visual Studio IDE, enabling developers to create and execute test scripts within the IDE and ensuring that their apps scale and perform as needed. Features include point and click scalability testing, the ability to validate responses, and functionality to test Web apps and perform functional Web testing.

Visual Studio also includes a low-level performance analysis tool, Visual Studio Analyzer, for identifying and fixing application bottlenecks. It has been updated for this release to include new support for capturing and raising industry standard Windows Management Instrumentation (WMI) events and the ability to modify tests while they are running.

The deployment phase for distributed applications can be difficult. As any developer who has built a distributed Web solution knows, these applications can be difficult to set up and deploy. Often server resources like message queues or performance counters need to exist on a middle-tier server before an application can run. However, included in the new tools in Visual Studio, there is a setup tool focused on distributing all tiers of a distributed application. You can build a setup that will deploy to logical machines that can in turn map to multiple physical machines. You'll also be able to build post-deployment debugging and functionality changes right into your applications.

When you build an application for Windows with the new multitier deployment projects in Visual Studio.NET, your application requires no setup. You simply point to the location of the application and run it. Additionally, applications built with Visual Studio.NET are self-repairing. If a user accidentally deletes a DLL or the application itself, it will automatically be replaced by the system. Visual Studio will include the next version of AppCenter to aid deployment to server farms and allow distributed application management with graphical tools.

Conclusion

The new features of Visual Studio.NET make it a complete development environment for building on the Microsoft .NET Framework, Microsoft's next generation Web application development platform. It provides key enabling technologies to simplify the creation, deployment, and ongoing evolution of secure, reliable, scalable, highly available Web Services while using existing developer skills. In addition, the framework provides features to help Web developers use Web Services as if they were local objects in the developers' preferred development language to simplify service and app development, and let developers focus their time and efforts on the unique services that give their company a competitive advantage. The result is faster time to market, improved developer productivity, and ultimately higher quality software.

Unified IDE Maximizes Developer Productivity

This article was published in fall 2000 on MSDN Online. With Visual Studio.NET, Microsoft builds on its reputation for providing the most productive tools for developers. Visual Studio.NET offers a single shared integrated development environment for all the languages within it. Thanks to such features as AutoHide, Dockable Windows, Tabbed Documents, Favorites, and Multimonitor Support, Visual Studio.NET makes it easier than ever for developers to view more of their code on screen at one time. Visual Studio.NET provides a Web Forms Designer, a Windows Forms Designer, a Component Designer, and an XML Designer. Visual Studio.NET also comes equipped with Visual Studio Macros, which allows developers to quickly customize the behavior of Visual Studio.NET to fit their individual needs. Finally, instead of requiring multiple tools for creating database schemas, stored procedures, indexes, triggers, and other items, developers will be able to perform these tasks within the Visual Studio.NET IDE.

Historically, Microsoft has been known for providing the most productive tools for developers. With Visual Studio.NET, Microsoft builds on this legacy, delivering a true developer cockpit that will dramatically increase developer productivity. The key features of Visual Studio.NET include:

- Shared Integrated Development Environment
- Window Management
- Designers
- Visual Studio Macros
- Visual Database Tools

Shared Integrated Development Environment

Microsoft Visual Studio.NET sports a single shared integrated development environment (IDE) for all the languages within it. It was designed to help developers build their solutions faster with less clutter and with all of the tools easily accessible in any of the languages in the Visual Studio® development system. The Visual Studio.NET IDE has a host of features that bring developers information when they need it and how they want it.

Start Page

Each time a developer launches Visual Studio, the Start Page is displayed. The default Web browser home page for the IDE, it provides a central location for setting preferred options, reading product news, accessing discussions with fellow developers, and obtaining other information to get up and running within the Visual Studio.NET environment (see Figure 1).

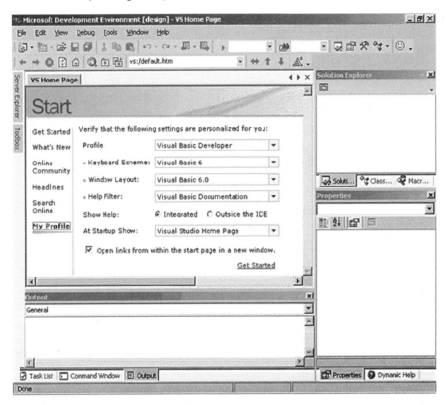

Figure 1. The Visual Studio Start Page is a developer portal

In addition to providing instant access to articles, events, and help topics from MSDN® Online, the Start Page allows developers to access existing and new projects with the click of a button. The Start Page also enables developers to quickly customize the look and feel of the IDE based on their development experience. This allows Microsoft Visual Basic® and Visual C++® developers to instantly set the Visual Studio.NET keyboard mapping scheme, window layout, and help topics to those already familiar to them.

Solution Explorer

Solution Explorer displays an organized list of projects as well as the corresponding files and directories that are part of the current solution (see Figure 2). Solution Explorer provides developers with an intuitive view of all files in a given project, saving time when editing large, complex projects.

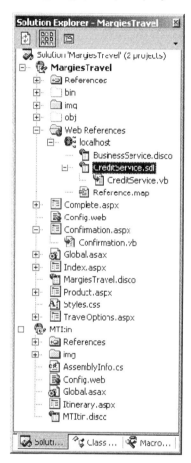

Figure 2. Solution Explorer displays the hierarchy of all projects and corresponding files in a given solution

Enhanced Toolbox

The Toolbox window displays a variety of items for use in Visual Studio projects. The items available from this window change depending upon which designer or editor the developer is using. Items displayed can include Web and Windows®-based form controls, ActiveX® controls, Web Services, Hypertext Markup Language (HTML) elements, objects, and items from the Windows Clipboard.

The Visual Studio.NET Toolbox has been enhanced to improve developer productivity. In addition to offering new components for Web Forms, Windows Forms, and data development, Visual Studio.NET allows code snippets to be highlighted in the Code Window and dragged onto the Toolbox for later reuse.

Server Explorer

Server Explorer is a new server-development console for Visual Studio.NET. It is a shared tool window that helps developers access and manipulate resources on any computer for which they have permission. With Server Explorer, developers can connect to servers and view their resources including message queues, performance counters, services, processes, event logs, and database objects.

In addition, Server Explorer enables developers to programmatically reference these server components and resources within their Visual Studio.NET applications, either by adding a component to their project that references the resource or by creating components that monitor the resource's activity. This includes making data connections to Microsoft SQL Server or other databases; configuring and integrating Microsoft Exchange 2000 into an application; monitoring processes, services, and dynamic-link libraries (DLLs) loaded on a server; and debugging server events.

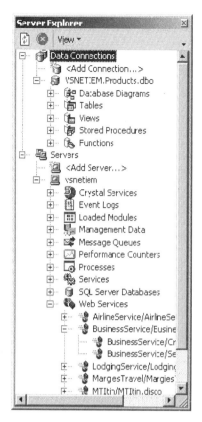

Figure 3. Server Explorer helps developers access Web Services, databases, message queues, and server event logs

Finally, Server Explorer gives developers direct access to all available Web Services on a particular server. Using Server Explorer, developers have the ability to view information about the methods and schemas that Web Services make available, and can instantly set references to the services for use in an application.

Task List

In addition to writing code and creating the components that make up an application, developers must be able to annotate their code so that, when they or other team members open it later in the development cycle, the exact state of the code can be determined without delay. The Visual Studio.NET Task List provides this crucial capability to developers by allowing them to mark their code with specialized comments. These comments then are parsed and displayed in a tabular format within the Task List (see Figure 4). In addition to the default TODO statement, developers can customize which "tags" the Task List parses.

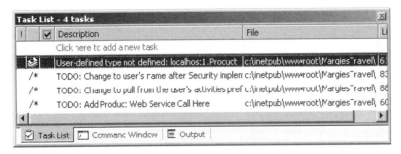

Figure 4. The Task List lets developers annotate their code so that they can keep track of areas that need attention

The Task List also serves as a central location where developers can ascertain the status of compile/build errors and warnings. With the Task List window, developers can identify and locate problems that are detected automatically as they edit and compile code. Double-clicking the task jumps the developer directly to the section of code containing the comment. Checking off the task removes the comment altogether. Developers also can filter the task items they view so that they see only the items they are interested in.

Dynamic Help

The Dynamic Help window provides one-click access to pertinent help regardless of the task a developer is attempting to complete. By tracking the selections a developer makes, the placement of the cursor, and the items in focus within the IDE, Dynamic Help filters through topics available on MSDN Online and provides pointers to relevant information specific to the current development task at hand.

Document Windows

Enhanced IntelliSense

To make the writing of Web pages easier and less prone to errors, IntelliSense® technology has been enhanced to handle not only compiled languages but also HTML and Extensible Markup Language (XML). This enables Web developers to get immediate information on available tags, properties, and even values within the code editor. Using IntelliSense within an application, developers gain all the benefits of automatic statement completion and syntax notification as they write their code.

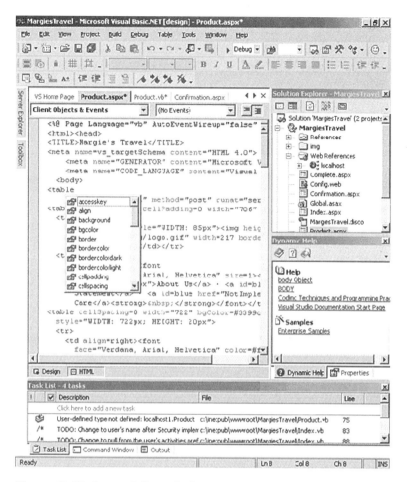

Figure 5. Statement Completion suggests ways to finish a line of code, saving developers the hassle of learning all of the intricacies of a given object

Enhanced Integrated Debugger

Visual Studio.NET contains an enhanced integrated debugger that shortens the development cycle by giving developers an easy way to run, track, and fix errors in their code. Developers can set conditional breakpoints that offer the fastest way to track down programming errors by stopping application execution only when a specified condition is met. Visual Studio.NET offers powerful conditional breakpoint options such as hit counts and per-thread tracking. Also, these breakpoints can be saved as part of a solution in Visual Studio.NET.

The Visual Studio.NET debugger supports debugging of applications written in multiple languages. Cross-language debugging allows developers to step seamlessly between Visual Basic, Visual C++, C#, Managed Extensions for C++, HTML, and script. Cross-language call stacks make it easy to debug components written in multiple languages.

Visual Studio.NET also offers a complete range of cross-process debugging. Because today's applications are increasingly distributed solutions, developers need a way to step remotely from client calls into server calls. In Visual Studio.NET, cross-process debugging allows developers to step instantly from any client-side call to any server-side call. Cross-process debugging works in Web-based solutions such as HTML-hosted applications and in straightforward Windows-based applications.

In addition, the Visual Studio.NET debugger has the ability to attach to a program that is running outside Visual Studio. Developers can use this capability to debug programs not created in Visual Studio, debug multiple programs simultaneously, or debug applications running on a remote computer.

Command Window

The Command Window provides developers with a flexible mechanism to quickly execute Visual Studio commands directly in the Visual Studio.NET environment. Within the window, developers have keyboard access to all commands that may be issued within the IDE. The Command Window enables developers to directly interact with the IDE, bypassing the menu system, executing commands that don't appear in the menu, and avoiding dialog boxes by using command parameters, switches, and arguments.

Window Management

In addition to the new integrated development environment, Visual Studio.NET makes it easier than ever to view more of your code on screen at one time.

Auto Hide

Auto Hide allows you to "hide" tool windows, such as Solution Explorer and Toolbox, along the edges of the IDE so that the windows do not occupy valuable space. To view the hidden window, developers simply place the mouse over the appropriate tab and the window will be displayed. They can also toggle an on/off "pin" to enable or disable Auto Hide for each window.

Dockable Windows

To help developers maintain a less cluttered workspace, all of the various information windows are dockable. Windows can be dragged around the workspace and attached to other windows, forced into a "tab linked" mode with other windows, or even allowed to remain freestanding.

Tabbed Documents

This feature automatically tabs document windows together within the IDE. For example, when developers edit multiple documents in the editor or designer, the documents all appear in the editor as tabs at the top.

IDE Navigation

Back and Forward buttons allow developers to navigate through the open windows in the environment, as well as the selection and cursor history within files, in much the same way that Back and Forward work in Web browsers. For example, if developers edit code on line 12 and then moved to line 102, they can use the Back button to quickly return to the same location in line 12. Both the Back and Forward buttons have a drop-down list that displays the navigation history.

Favorites

Developers now can access their Web browser Favorites and add links to the Favorites list from within Visual Studio.

Multimonitor Support

Visual Studio.NET provides support for multiple monitors so that developers can have more windows open at the same time without sacrificing screen space.

Designers

Web Form Designer

Today's developers need an intuitive way to create Web pages. Visual Studio.NET includes the shared Visual Studio Web Form Designer, a graphical way to develop HTML pages, Active Server Pages, and ASP.NET Web Forms without delving into HTML or script code. For detailed information about Web Forms and building Web applications in Visual Studio.NET, see Visual Studio Enables the Programmable Web.

Windows Forms Designer

Windows Forms provide a concise, object-oriented, extensible set of classes that enable developers to quickly develop rich Windows-based applications. Using the Windows Forms Designer, developers rapidly can develop solutions for use in Windows-based applications. By simply adding a new form to a project, the developer has a basis from which to quickly create rich, intuitive user interfaces. Once a Windows Form has been added to a Visual Studio.NET solution, the developer can set form properties, add controls from the Toolbox, and write code behind the form. For a detailed discussion of Windows Forms, see Introducing Windows Forms.

Component Designer

In the same way that form designers enable rapid creation of client applications, Visual Studio.NET provides a way to build server-side components quickly and graphically. The Component Designer applies the concepts of rapid application development (RAD) form-based programming to building middle-tier objects-a visual way for building nonvisual objects. Instead of writing lots of server-based code, developers can drag and drop server components to a design surface that will run on the server. Just double-click a server component on the Component Designer, and the code for that object is opened.

XML Designer

The XML Designer provides intuitive tools for working with XML and XML Schema Definition (XSD) files. Within the designer, there are three views: one for creating and editing XSD schemas, one for structured editing of XML data files, and one for editing XML source code.

The Schema view provides a visual design surface on which developers can visually construct and edit XML schemas. New schemas can be created in the designer by adding new elements, types, and attributes to the editor, or by dragging tables onto the design surface from Server Explorer. In addition, the Schema view allows developers to create relationships between tables and generate ADO.NET datasets.

The Data view is available when an XML data file is added to a Visual Studio.NET project. Using the Data view, developers can generate, reference, and view a schema associated with an XML file. Developers can also view and edit data using the Data view, making it simple to work directly with XML-based data as if it were in a database.

The XML Source view provides an editor for creating and editing XML. This view offers developers IntelliSense technology and statement completion for XML files that are associated with a specified schema.

Visual Studio Macros

Visual Studio.NET comes equipped with a rich extensibility model for customizing, automating, and extending the integrated development environment. To best leverage this extensibility model from within the IDE, Visual Studio.NET provides the Visual Studio Macros environment.

This environment, built on Visual Studio technology and invoked by pressing ALT+F11, allows developers to rapidly customize the behavior of Visual Studio.NET to fit their individual needs. Using Visual Studio Macros, developers can automate repetitive processes to save time and effort, much like Microsoft Office developers do today using Visual Basic for Applications. In addition, Visual Studio Macros enable developers to record macros that can later be played back to automate processes within the IDE.

Visual Database Tools

Visual Studio.NET includes comprehensive features for working with databases to maximize developer productivity. Instead of requiring multiple tools for creating database schemas, stored procedures, indexes, triggers, and other items, developers can perform these tasks within the Visual Studio.NET IDE. Let's take a closer look at some of the features provided with the Visual Database Tools in Visual Studio.

Database Designer

Developers can work easily and quickly with physical database schemas for Microsoft SQL Server and Oracle using the Database Designer. The Database Designer provides a visual view of the schema and can be edited directly to add, modify, or remove tables, columns, indexes, views, and other database objects. In addition, relationships between tables can be viewed and modified, providing complete control over the physical database design. With the Database Designer, developers have the power to work with SQL Server and Oracle database schemas without leaving Visual Studio.

Query Designer

The Query Designer enables developers to create complex SQL queries quickly and easily. Developers can create their query visually and then directly edit the corresponding SQL script with complete fidelity between the script and visual diagram. The results from the query can be viewed to verify correctness, making it much faster for developers to work with data.

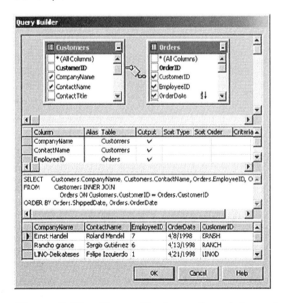

Figure 6. The Query Designer is a rich surface for designing and testing SQL queries

Database Project

Visual Studio.NET includes database projects so that developers can group all of the elements relating to their data in one place, including change and create scripts and any queries they may have.

Script Editor

Developers easily can work with stored procedures, triggers, or any SQL script using the Script Editor. Color-coded syntax makes it easy to view SQL keywords. The Query Designer can be easily invoked for visually designing a code block by right-clicking a Select statement.

Stored Procedure Debugging

Visual Studio.NET includes seamless stored procedure debugging for developers using Microsoft SQL Server version 6.5 or higher. This makes it simple for developers to step right from business logic code into the SQL statements, decreasing the time to fix any bugs.

Conclusion

Visual Studio.NET provides a single shared development environment that helps developers build their solutions faster and with access to key productivity regardless of the language used. The Visual Studio.NET IDE is a completely customizable cockpit that enables the highest performance for developers.

Preparing Your Visual Basic 6.0 Applications for the Upgrade to Visual Basic.NET

This article was published in October 2000 on MSDN Online. Visual Basic.NET will open and upgrade Visual Basic 6.0 projects to Visual Basic.NET technologies, but in most cases, developers will need to make some modifications to their projects after bringing them into Visual Basic.NET. After a project has been upgraded, an upgrade report is added to the project, itemizing any changes that will need to be made to the upgraded code. Furthermore, comments are added to the code to alert the developer to any potential problems. The .NET platform improves upon previous architectures and adds greater support for scalability and distributed applications. To best take advantage of these features, developers should design their applications with architecture similar to that which they would use in Visual Basic.NET. The author provides recommendations for how developers should write code to minimize the changes that they will need to make after upgrading a project to Visual Basic.NET.

Overview

This document provides recommendations for developers using Microsoft Visual Basic who are planning to upgrade their applications to Microsoft Visual Basic.NET.

Visual Basic.NET will open and upgrade Visual Basic 6.0 projects to Visual Basic.NET technologies, but in most cases you will need to make some modifications to your projects after bringing them into Visual Basic.NET. The purpose of this document is to recommend how to design and implement your current Visual Basic projects to minimize the number of changes you will need to make when they are upgraded to Visual Basic.NET. Where appropriate, we use new language constructs; however, this document is not intended to be a Visual Basic.NET language reference.

Note Visual Basic.NET is still in development; some compatibility details may change before the product is released. Following the guidelines in this document does not guarantee your code will not require changes; instead the guidelines aim to reduce the amount of work needed for conversion.

The upgrade wizard and command-line upgrade tools in Visual Basic.NET are still in an early stage of development and, as such, their functionality is limited. The purpose of including them in the Beta release is to give you a feel for how the upgrade process will work and to see how VB 6.0 code is modified to work in VB.NET; in Beta1, most real-world projects probably cannot be migrated successfully.

What Is Visual Basic.NET?

Visual Basic.NET is the next version of Visual Basic. Rather than simply adding some new features to Visual Basic 6.0, Microsoft has reengineered the product to make it easier than ever before to write distributed applications such as Web and enterprise n-tier systems. Visual Basic.NET has two new forms packages (Windows Forms and Web Forms); a new version of ADO for accessing disconnected data sources; and streamlined language, removing legacy keywords, improving type safety, and exposing low-level constructs that advanced developers require.

These new features open new doors for the Visual Basic developer: With Web Forms and ADO.NET, you can now rapidly develop scalable Web sites; with inheritance, the language now truly supports object-oriented programming; Windows Forms natively supports accessibility and visual inheritance; and deploying your applications is now as simple as copying your executables and components from directory to directory.

Visual Basic.NET is now fully integrated with the other Microsoft Visual Studio.NET languages. Not only can you develop application components in different programming languages, your classes can now inherit from classes written in other languages using cross-language inheritance. With the unified debugger, you can now debug multiple language applications, irrespective of whether they are running locally or on remote computers. Finally, whatever language you use, the Microsoft .NET Framework provides a rich set of APIs for Microsoft Windows and the Internet.

Why Is Visual Basic.NET Not 100% Compatible?

There were two options to consider when designing Visual Basic.NETretrofit the existing code base to run on top of the .NET Framework, or build from the ground up, taking full advantage of the platform. To deliver the features most requested by customers (for example, inheritance, threading), to provide full and uninhibited access to the platform, and to ensure that Visual Basic moves forward into the next generation of Web applications, the right decision was to build from the ground up on the new platform.

For example, many of the new features found in Windows Forms could have been added to the existing code base as new controls or more properties. However, this would have been at the cost of all the other great features inherent to Windows Forms, such as security and visual inheritance.

One of our major goals was to ensure Visual Basic code could fully interoperate with code written in other languages, such as Microsoft Visual C# or Microsoft Visual C++, and enable the Visual Basic developer to harness the power of the .NET Framework simply, without resorting to the programming workarounds traditionally required to make Windows APIs work. Visual Basic now has the same variable types, arrays, user-defined types, classes, and interfaces as Visual C++ and any other language that targets the Common Language Runtime; however, we had to remove some features, such as fixed-length strings and non-zero based arrays from the language.

Visual Basic is now a true object-oriented language; some unintuitive and inconsistent features like **GoSub/Return** and **DefInt** have been removed from the language.

The result is a re-energized Visual Basic, which will continue to be the most productive tool for creating Windows-based applications, and is now positioned to be the best tool for creating the next generation Web sites.

Upgrading to Visual Basic.NET

Visual Basic.NET enables a fundamental shift from traditional Windows development to building next-generation Web and n-tier applications. For this reason, your code will need to be upgraded to take advantage of Visual Basic.NET.

This happens automatically when you open a Visual Basic 6.0 project in Visual Basic.NET: the Upgrade Wizard steps you through the upgrade process and creates a new Visual Basic.NET project (your existing project is left unchanged). This is a one-way process; the new Visual Basic.NET project cannot be opened in Visual Basic 6.0.

When your project is upgraded, the language is modified for any syntax changes and your Visual Basic 6.0 Forms are converted to Windows Forms. In most cases, you will have to make some changes to your code after it is upgraded. This is required because certain objects and language features either have no equivalent in Visual Basic.NET, or have an equivalent too dissimilar for an automatic upgrade. After the upgrade, you may also want to change your application to take advantage of some of the new features in Visual Basic.NET.

For example, Windows Forms supports control anchoring, so you can remove most of your old Visual Basic 6.0 Form resize code:

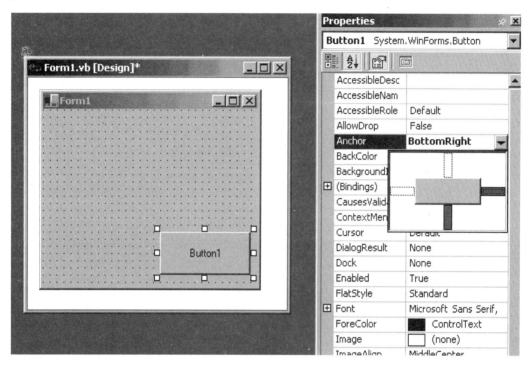

Figure 1. VB.NET support for control anchoring

To help you make the changes, after your project is upgraded, Visual Basic.NET adds an "upgrade report" to your project itemizing any problems, and inserts comments into your upgraded code alerting you to statements that will need to be changed. Because these comments are displayed as "TO DO" tasks in the new Task List window, you can easily see what changes are required, and navigate to the code statement simply by double-clicking the task. Each task and item in the upgrade report is associated with an online Help topic giving further guidance as to why the code needs to be changed, and what you need to do.

By following the recommendations in this document, you can minimize and, in some cases, eliminate the changes needed after upgrading your project to Visual Basic.NET. In most cases, the recommendations simply represent good programming practices; however, we also identify the objects and methods which have no equivalents, and which should be used sparingly if you intend to upgrade your project to Visual Basic.NET.

Working with Both Visual Basic 6.0 and Visual Basic.NET

Visual Basic.NET supports upgrading Visual Basic 6.0 projects; if you have a project written in Visual Basic versions 1 to 5, we recommend you load it into VB6 (choosing to upgrade Microsoft ActiveX controls), compile, and save the project before upgrading it to Visual Basic.NET.

Both Visual Basic.NET and Visual Basic 6.0 can be installed on the same computer and run at the same time. Likewise, applications written in Visual Basic.NET and Visual Basic 6.0 can be installed and executed on the same computer. Components written in Visual Basic.NET can interoperate with COM components written in earlier versions of Visual Basic and other languages. For example, you can drop an ActiveX control written in Visual Basic 6.0 onto a Visual Basic.NET Windows Form, use a Visual Basic 6.0 COM object from a Visual Basic.NET class library, or add a reference to a Visual Basic.NET library to a Visual Basic 6.0 executable.

Components compiled with Visual Basic.NET have subtle run-time differences from components compiled with Visual Basic 6.0. For starters, because Visual Basic.NET objects are released through garbage collection, when objects are explicitly destroyed, there may be a lag before they are actually removed from memory. There are additional differences such as the variant/object changes described later in this document. The combined result of these differences is that Visual Basic.NET applications will have similar but not identical run-time behavior to Visual Basic 6.0 applications.

In addition, Visual Basic.NET makes binary compatibility between Visual Basic.NET components and those in Visual Basic 6.0 unnecessary. Components now have a more robust versioning and deployment system than ever before, files can be deployed by simply copying to a directory (no more RegSvr32), and upgrading to a new version of a component is as simple as replacing the old file with a new file. All you have to do is ensure classes and methods are compatible with the previous version.

Architecture Recommendations

The .NET platform improves upon previous architectures, and adds greater support for scalability and distributed applications though disconnected data access, HTTP-based message transport, and file-copy based deployment (no more registering of components). To best take advantage of these features, you should design your applications with an architecture similar to that you would use in Visual Basic.NET.

Browser-based Applications

Visual Basic 6.0 and Microsoft Visual Studio 6.0 offered several technologies for creating browser-based Internet and intranet applications:

- Webclasses
- DHTML projects
- ActiveX documents
- Active Server Pages (ASP)

Visual Basic.NET introduces ASP.NET, an enhanced version of ASP, and adds to the architecture with Web Forms, which are HTML pages with Visual Basic events. The architecture is server-based.

Below is a list of recommendations and architectural suggestions for developing Visual Basic 6.0 browser-based applications that will most seamlessly migrate to Visual Basic.NET projects:

- We recommend you use the Microsoft multi-tier architecture guidelines to create your applications, create the interface with ASP, and use Visual Basic 6.0 or Visual C++ 6.0 COM objects for your business logic. ASP is fully supported in Visual Basic.NET, and you can continue to extend your application using ASP, ASP.NET, and Web Forms. The Visual Basic 6.0 and Visual C++ 6.0 business objects can either be used without modification or upgraded to Visual Studio.NET.

- DHTML applications contain DHTML pages and client-side DLLs. These applications cannot be automatically upgraded to Visual Basic.NET. We recommend you leave these applications in Visual Basic 6.0.

- ActiveX documents are not supported in Visual Basic.NET, and like DHTML projects, cannot be automatically upgraded. We recommend you either leave your ActiveX document applications in Visual Basic 6.0 or, where possible, replace ActiveX documents with user controls.

- Visual Basic 6.0 ActiveX documents and DHTML applications can interoperate with Visual Basic.NET technologies. For example, you can navigate from a Visual Basic.NET Web Form to a Visual Basic 6.0 DHTML page, and vice-versa.

- Webclasses no longer exist in Visual Basic.NET. Webclass applications will be upgraded to ASP.NET; however, you will have to make some modifications after upgrading. Existing Webclass applications can interoperate with Visual Basic.NET Web Forms and ASP applications, but for new projects we recommend you use the Windows DNA platform of ASP with Visual Basic 6.0 business objects.

For more information about building applications with the Microsoft multi-tier architecture, see the Microsoft Windows DNA Web site.

Client/Server Projects

Visual Basic 6.0 offered several technologies for creating client/server applications:

- Visual Basic Forms
- Microsoft Transaction Server (MTS)/COM+ middle-tier objects
- User controls

In Visual Basic.NET, there is a new form package: Windows Forms. Windows Forms has a different object model than Visual Basic 6.0 Forms, but is largely compatible. When your project is upgraded, Visual Basic Forms are converted to Windows Forms.

Visual Basic.NET improves support for developing middle-tier MTS and COM+ component services components. Using the unified debugger, you can step from a client application into an MTS/COM+ component and back to the client. You can also use the unified debugger to step through Visual Basic 6.0 MTS/COM+ components (providing they are compiled to native code, with symbolic debug information and no optimizations).

Visual Basic.NET also introduces a new middle-tier component, Web Services. Web Services are hosted by ASP.NET, and use the HTTP transport allowing method requests to pass through firewalls. They pass and return data using industry standard XML, allowing other languages and other platforms to access their functionality. Although they do not support MTS transactions, you may want to change your MTS/COM+ components to Web Services in cases where you do not need distributed transactions but still want to interoperate with other platforms. Although there is no automatic method for this, the task is trivial and can be completed in minutes using a drag-and-drop operation after your project has been upgraded to Visual Basic.NET.

When your project is upgraded, user controls are upgraded to Windows controls; however, custom property tag settings and accelerator keys assignments will not be upgraded.

Single-tier Applications

Visual Basic 6.0 supported building several types of single-tier applications:

- Single-tier database applications
- Visual Basic add-ins
- Utility programs and games

Single-tier database applications are typified by a Visual Basic application storing data in an Microsoft Access database. These applications will upgrade to Visual Basic.NET with some limitations (see the Data section later in this document).

Now that the Visual Basic.NET IDE is a fully integrated part of the Visual Studio.NET IDE, Visual Basic.NET has a new language-neutral extensibility model. Visual Basic.NET add-ins are now Visual Studio.NET add-ins, and you can automate and add features to any language in Visual Studio.NET. For example, you can write a Visual Basic.NET add-in that re-colors a Visual C# Windows Form or adds comments to a Visual Basic class. In order to provide this functionality, Visual Basic.NET has moved away from the old extensibility model, and you will need to change the extensibility objects in your application to take advantage of the new features.

Many applications fall under the category of Utility programs. Utility applications that manipulate files, registry settings, and the like will often upgrade without requiring any additional changes. After upgrading, there are many new features you can take advantage of, such as exception handling in the language to capture file system errors, and using .NET Framework registry classes to manipulate the registry. One thing to be aware of is that applications relying on specific performance characteristics of Visual Basic 6.0, such as arcade games, will probably require some modifications because Visual Basic.NET has different performance characteristics. For games support in Visual Basic.NET, you can use Microsoft DirectX 7, or the new version of GDI. GDI+ introduces many new features, including Alpha blending support for all 2-D graphics primitives, anti-aliasing, and expanded support for image file formats.

Data

Visual Basic 6.0 offered several types of data access:

- ActiveX Data Objects (ADO)
- Remote Data Objects (RDO)
- Data Access Objects (DAO)

Visual Basic.NET introduces an enhanced version of ADO called ADO.NET. ADO.NET targets disconnected data, and provides performance improvements over ADO when used in distributed applications. ADO.NET offers read/write data binding to controls for Windows Forms and read-only data binding for Web Forms.

DAO, RDO, and ADO can still be used in code from Visual Basic.NET, with some trivial modifications (covered in the language section of this document). However, Visual Basic.NET does not support DAO and RDO data binding to controls, data controls, or RDO User connection. We recommend that if your applications contain DAO or RDO data binding you either leave them in Visual Basic 6.0 or upgrade the DAO and RDO data binding to ADO before upgrading your project to Visual Basic.NET, as ADO data binding is supported in Windows Forms. Information on how to do this is available in the Visual Basic 6.0 Help.

In summary, we recommend using ADO in your Visual Basic 6.0 projects.

Upgrading

When your code is upgraded, Visual Basic.NET creates a new upgraded project and makes most of the required language and object changes for you. The following sections provide a few examples of how your code is upgraded.

Variant to Object

Previous versions of Visual Basic supported the **Variant** datatype, which could be assigned to any primitive type (except fixed-length strings), Empty, Error, Nothing and Null. In Visual Basic.NET, the functionality of the **Variant** and **Object** datatypes is combined into one new datatype: **Object**. The **Object** datatype can be assigned to primitive datatypes, Empty, Nothing, Null, and as a pointer to an object.

When your project is upgraded to Visual Basic.NET, all variables declared as **Variant** are changed to **Object**. Also, when code is inserted into the editor, the **Variant** keyword is replaced with **Object**.

Integer to Short

In Visual Basic.NET, the datatype for 16-bit whole numbers is now **Short**, and the datatype for 32-bit whole numbers is now **Integer** (**Long** is now 64 bits). When your project is upgraded, the variable types are changed:

```
Dim x As Integer
dim y as Long
```

is upgraded to:

```
Dim x As Short
dim y as Integer
```

Property Syntax

Visual Basic.NET introduces a more intuitive syntax for properties, which groups **Get** and **Set** together. Your property statements are upgraded as shown in the following example:

```
Property Get MyProperty() As Integer
    MyProperty = m_MyProperty
End Property
Property Let MyProperty(NewValue As Integer)
    m_MyProperty = NewValue
End Property
```

is upgraded to:

```
Property MyProperty() As Short
    Get
        MyProperty = m_MyProperty
    End Get
    Set
        m_MyProperty = Value
    End Set
End Property
```

Visual Basic Forms to Windows Forms

Visual Basic.NET has a new forms package, Windows Forms, which has native support for accessibility and has an in-place menu editor. Your existing Visual Basic Forms are upgraded to Windows Forms.

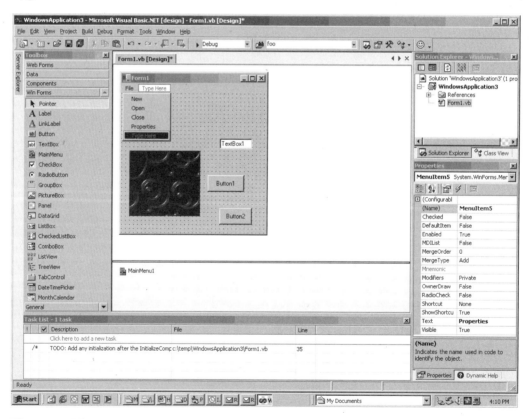

Figure 2. Windows Forms in-place menu editor.

Interfaces

In previous versions of Visual Basic, interfaces for public classes were always hidden from the user. In Visual Basic.NET, they can be viewed and edited in the Code Editor. When your project is upgraded, you choose whether to have interface declarations automatically created for your public classes.

Upgrade Report and Comments

After your project is upgraded, an upgrade report is added to your project, itemizing any changes you will need to make to your upgraded code. Additionally, comments are added to your code to alert you to any potential problems. These comments show up automatically in the Visual Studio.NET Task List.

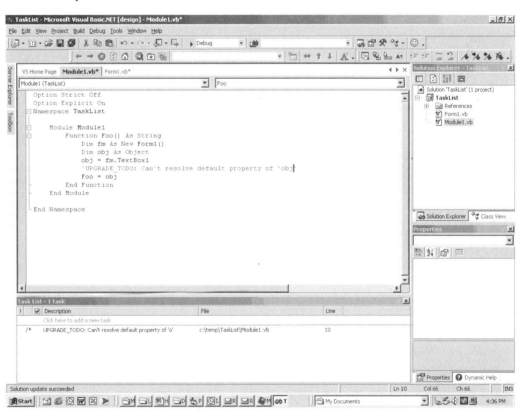

Figure 3. Upgrade comments are added to Visual Basic code as well as the Task List.

Programming Recommendations

This section provides recommendations for how you should write code to minimize the changes you will need to make after upgrading your project to Visual Basic.NET.

Use Early-Binding

Both Visual Basic 6.0 and Visual Basic.NET support late-bound objects, which is the practice of declaring a variable as the **Object** datatype and assigning it to an instance of a class at run time. However, during the upgrade process, late-bound objects can introduce problems when resolving default properties, or in cases where the underlying object model has changed and properties, methods, and events need to be converted. For example, suppose you have a Form called Form1 with a label called Label1; the following Visual Basic 6.0 code would set the caption of the label to "SomeText":

```
Dim o As Object
Set o = Me.Label1
o.Caption = "SomeText"
```

In Visual Basic.NET Windows Forms, the **Caption** property of a label control is now called **Text**. When your code is upgraded, all instances of the **Caption** property are changed to **Text**, but because a late-bound object is type-less, Visual Basic cannot detect what type of object it is, or if any properties should be translated. In such cases, you will need to change the code yourself after upgrading.

If you rewrite the code using early-bound objects, it will be upgraded automatically:

```
Dim o As Label
Set o = Me.Label1
o.Caption = "SomeText"
```

Where possible you should declare variables of the appropriate object type rather than simply declaring them as the **Object** datatype.

In the cases where you do use Object and Variant variables in your Visual Basic 6.0 code, we recommend you use explicit conversions when you assign the variables, perform operations on the variables, or pass the variables to a function. For example, the intention of the "+" operation in the following code is unclear:

```
Dim Var1 As Variant
Dim Var2 As Variant
Dim Var3 As Variant
Var1 = "3"
Var2 = 4
Var3 = Var1 + Var2    'UNCLEAR: What is the intention?
```

Should Var1 and Var2 be added as strings or integers?

The above example may result in a run-time error in Visual Basic.NET. Rewriting the final line to use explicit conversions ensures the code will work:

```
Var3 = CInt(Var1) + CInt(Var2)   'GOOD: explicit conversion
```

Visual Basic.NET supports overloading functions based on parameter type.
For example, the **Environ** function now has two forms:

```
Environ( Expression As Integer) As String
Environ( Expression As String ) As String
```

Visual Basic.NET determines which function to call based on the parameter type. If you pass an integer to **Environ()**, the integer version is called; if you pass a string, then the string version is called. Code that passes a **Variant** or **Object** datatype to an overloaded function may cause a compile or runtime error. Using an explicit conversion, as in the following example, will mean your code will work as intended after it is upgraded to Visual Basic.NET:

```
Dim a As String
Dim v As Variant
v = "Path"
a = Environ(CStr(v)) 'GOOD: explicit conversion
```

Using explicit conversions of late bound objects is good coding practice. It makes the intention of the code easy to determine, and makes it easier for you to move your project to Visual Basic.NET.

Use Date for Storing Dates

Earlier versions of Visual Basic supported using the **Double** datatype to store and manipulate dates. You should not do this in Visual Basic.NET, because dates are not internally stored as doubles. For example, the following is valid in Visual Basic 6.0, but may cause a compile error in Visual Basic.NET:

```
Dim dbl As Double
Dim dat As Date
dat = Now
dbl = dat       'VB.NET: Double can't be assigned to a date
dbl = DateAdd("d", 1, dbl)'VB.NET: Can't use Double in date functions
dat = CDate(dbl) 'VB.NET: CDate can't convert double to date
```

The .NET framework provides the **ToOADate** and **FromOADate** functions to convert between doubles and dates. However, when your project is upgraded to Visual Basic.NET, it is difficult to determine the intention of code that uses doubles to store dates. To avoid unnecessary modifications to your code in Visual Basic.NET, always use the **Date** datatype to store dates.

Resolve Parameterless Default Properties

In Visual Basic 6.0, many objects expose default properties, which can be omitted as a programming shortcut. For example, **TextBox** has a default property of **Text**, so instead of writing:

```
MsgBox Form1.Text1.Text
```

you use the shortcut:

```
MsgBox Form1.Text1
```

The default property is resolved when the code is compiled. In addition, you could also use default properties with late-bound objects, as in the following example:

```
Dim obj As Object
Set obj = Form1.Text1
MsgBox obj
```

In the late-bound example, the default property is resolved at run time, and the **MsgBox** displays the value of the default property of the **TextBox** as **Text1**.

Visual Basic.NET does not support parameterless default properties, and consequently does not allow this programming shortcut. When your project is upgraded, Visual Basic.NET resolves the parameterless default properties, but late-bound usages that rely on run-time resolution cannot be automatically resolved. In these cases, you will have to change the code yourself. An additional complication is that many libraries implement default properties using a property called **_Default**. **_Default** acts as a proxy, passing calls to the real default property. So, when your project is upgraded, some default properties will be resolved to **_Default**. The code will still work as usual, but it will be less understandable than code written explicitly using the actual property. For these reasons, try to avoid using parameterless default properties in your Visual Basic 6.0 code. Instead of writing:

```
Dim obj As Object
Set obj = Me.Text1
MsgBox obj       'Relying on default property
MsgBox Me.Text1  'Relying on default property
```

use:

```
Dim obj As Object
Set obj = Me.Text1
MsgBox obj.Text   'GOOD: Default property is resolved
MsgBox Me.Text1.Text 'GOOD: Default property is resolved
```

While *parameterless* default properties are not supported in Visual Basic.NET, default properties *with parameters* are supported. To understand the difference between the two types, consider that parametered default properties always have an index. An example is the default property of ADO **recordset**: the **Fields** collection.

The code:

```
Dim rs As ADODB.Recordset
rs("CompanyName") = "SomeCompany"
rs!CompanyName = "SomeCompany"
```

is actually a shortcut for:

```
Dim rs As ADODB.Recordset
rs.Fields("CompanyName").Value = "SomeCompany"
rs.Fields!CompanyName.Value = "SomeCompany"
```

In this case, the **Fields** property is parametered, and so the usage is valid in Visual Basic.NET; however, the default property of the **Fields** property, **Value,** is parameterless, so the correct usage in Visual Basic.NET is:

```
Dim rs As ADODB.Recordset
rs("CompanyName").Value = "SomeCompany"
rs!CompanyName.Value = "SomeCompany"
```

This example and most other default properties are resolved for you when the project is upgraded, so resolving them in Visual Basic 6.0 is simply a good programming practice. However, you should avoid using default properties with the **Object** and **Variant** datatypes, as these cannot be resolved and you will have to fix the code yourself in the upgraded project.

Use Boolean Comparisons with AND/OR/NOT

The **And** and **Or** keywords work differently in Visual Basic.NET than in Visual Basic 6.0. In Visual Basic 6.0, the **And** keyword performed a logical **AND** as well as a Bitwise **AND** depending on the types of the operands (due to **True** having a value of –1). In Visual Basic.NET, **AND** only performs a logical **AND**. In Visual Basic.NET, a new set of operators have been added to the language to perform Bitwise operations: **BitAnd**, **BitOr**, **BitNot**, and **BitXor**.

The following example demonstrates the effect of this difference:

```
Dim a As Integer
Dim b As Integer
Dim c As Boolean
a = 1
b = 2
c = a And b
MsgBox ("The answer is " & c)
```

When this code is run in Visual Basic 6.0, the answer is **False** (Bitwise **AND**); however, in Visual Basic.NET, the answer is **True** (logical **AND**). In order to ensure that your code still behaves the same after it has been upgraded, Visual Basic.NET includes the compatibility functions **VB6.And**, **VB6.Or**, and **VB6.Not**, which evaluate **AND/OR/NOT** in the same way Visual Basic 6.0 did (choosing logical or Bitwise depending on the operands). When the above code is upgraded, the result will look similar to the following:

```
Dim a As Short
Dim b As Short
Dim c As Boolean
a = 1
b = 2
c = VB6.And(a, b)
MsgBox ("The answer is " & c)
```

The upgraded code will produce the answer **False**, just as the original did in Visual Basic 6.0.

To prevent your code from being upgraded to the compatibility functions, try to ensure that your **AND/OR/NOT** statements use Boolean comparisons. For example, if the above example is modified to:

```
Dim a As Integer
Dim b As Integer
Dim c As Boolean
a = 1
b = 2
c = a <> 0 And b <> 0
MsgBox ("The answer is " & c)
```

then after the project upgrade, the resulting code will be more familiar:

```
Dim a As Short
Dim b As Short
Dim c As Boolean
a = 1
b = 2
c = a <> 0 And b <> 0
MsgBox ("The answer is " & c)
```

The difference is that each operator being compared is a Boolean expression, and therefore uses the logical **AND** in Visual Basic 6.0. Logical **AND** produces the same result in both Visual Basic 6.0 and Visual Basic.NET so the code is left unchanged. Doing this means you can cut and paste code between Visual Basic.NET and Visual Basic 6.0, and your code will execute more quickly in Visual Basic.NET because it is using the native **AND** operator instead of a compatibility function.

Visual Basic.NET handles functions in **AND/OR/NOT** operations differently than Visual Basic 6.0. Consider the following example:

```
Dim b As Boolean
b = Function1() And Function2()
```

In Visual Basic 6.0, both **Function1** and **Function2** are evaluated. In Visual Basic.NET, **Function2** is only evaluated if **Function1** returns **True**. This is known as *short-circuiting* of logical operators. In most cases the only run-time difference is that the short-circuited version executes more quickly; however, if **Function2** has side effects, such as manipulating a database or a global variable, then the statement will have a different run-time behavior than in Visual Basic 6.0. To prevent this problem, if your **AND/OR/NOT** statements contain functions, methods, or properties then the statement is upgraded to a compatibility version that evaluates the functions. The above example would be upgraded to the following:

```
Dim b As Boolean
b = VB6.AND(Function1(), Function2())
```

To prevent your code from being upgraded to the compatibility version, make the following modifications:

```
Dim b As Boolean
Dim c As Boolean
Dim d As Boolean
c = Function1()
d = Function2()
b = c And d
```

It is also important to note that in Visual Basic.NET, the underlying value of **True** has been changed from −1 to 1. This change was made to help Visual Basic applications interoperate with the other .NET languages, and finally resolves a major disparity with Visual C++. Because of this change, in your Visual Basic 6.0 applications, you should always use the constant **True** instead of -1, and Boolean types instead of integers to hold Boolean values. To illustrate the importance of this, consider the following example, which produces the result **True** in Visual Basic 6.0, and **False** in Visual Basic.NET:

```
Dim i As Integer
i = True
If i = -1 Then
    MsgBox ("True")
Else
    MsgBox ("False")
End If
```

However, changing it to use Booleans generates the result **True** in both Visual Basic 6.0 and Visual Basic.NET, and also makes for more readable code:

```
Dim i As Boolean
i = True
If i = True Then
    MsgBox ("True")
Else
    MsgBox ("False")
End If
```

The most important things to remember and implement from this example are:

- Always use the constant names **True** and **False** instead of their underlying values 0 and −1.
- Use the Boolean datatype to store Boolean values.

If you do not do these two things, you may have to make many changes to your project after it has been upgraded to Visual Basic.NET.

Avoid Null Propagation

Previous versions of Visual Basic supported Null propagation. Null propagation supports the premise that when null is used in an expression, the result of the expression will itself be Null. In each case in the following example, the result of V is always Null.

```
Dim V
V = 1 + Null
V = Null + Right$("SomeText", 1)
V = Right("SomeText", 0)
```

Null propagation is not supported in Visual Basic.NET. The statement **1+Null** will generate a type mismatch in Visual Basic.NET. Additionally, where Visual Basic 6.0 had two versions of the **Left** function**Left$** returning a string, **Left** returning a variant which could be Null**Visual Basic.NET only has one version, **Left**, which always returns a string.

In order to be compatible with both Visual Basic 6.0 and Visual Basic.NET you should always write code to test for Null instead of relying on Null propagation. Furthermore, in Visual Basic.NET, the following functions will no longer return Null:

Chr	Environ	LTrim	RTrim	Trim
Command	Error	Mid	Space	UCase
CurDir	Hex	Oct	Str	
Date	LCase	Right	Time	

Null propagation is commonly used in database applications, where you need to check if a database field contains Null. In these cases you should check results using the function **IsNull()** and perform the appropriate action.

Use Zero Bound Arrays

Visual Basic 6.0 allowed you to define arrays with lower and upper bounds of any whole number. You could also use **ReDim** to reassign a variant as an array. To enable interoperability with other languages, arrays in Visual Basic.NET must have a lower bound of zero, and **ReDim** cannot be used unless the variable was previously declared with Dim As Array. Although this restricts the way arrays can be defined, it does allow you to pass arrays between Visual Basic.NET and any other .NET language. The following example shows the restriction:

```
Dim a(1 To 10) As Integer 'LBound must be 0 in VB.NET
Dim v
ReDim v(10) 'Can't use ReDim without Dim in VB.NET
Dim b(10) As Integer 'GOOD: Creates an array of 10 integers
ReDim b(5) As Integer   'GOOD: Can ReDim previously Dimed var
```

In addition, in Visual Basic 6.0, Dim (10) As Integer created an array of 11 integers, indexed from 0 to 10. The same statement in Visual Basic.NET creates an array of 10 integers, from 0 to 9.

A side effect is that Option Base 0|1 is removed from the language.

When your project is upgraded to Visual Basic.NET, any option base statements are removed from your code. If the array is zero bound, it is left unchanged. However, if an array is non-zero bound, then it is upgraded to an array wrapper class, as in the following example:

```
Dim a(1 To 10) As Integer
```

changes to:

```
Dim a As Object = New VB6.Array(GetType(Short), 1,10)
```

The array wrapper class is much slower than the native array, and there are limitations with using the two array types in the same application. For example, you cannot pass a wrapper array to some functions that take parameters of type Array, and you may not be able to pass a wrapper array to a Visual C# or Visual C++ class.

For this reason, you should use zero bound arrays in your Visual Basic 6.0 code, avoid using **ReDim** as an array declaration, and avoid using Option Base 1.

Use Constants Instead of Underlying Values

When writing code, try to use constants rather than relying on their underlying values. For example, if you are maximizing a form at run time, use:

```
Me.WindowState = vbMaximized 'Good: Constant name used
```

rather than:

```
Me.WindowStyle = 2   'Avoid using underlying value
Me.WindowStyle = X   'Avoid using variables
```

Likewise, use **True** and **False** instead of -1 and 0.

In Visual Basic.NET, the values and in some cases the names of some properties and constants have changed; for example, the value of **True** changes from -1 to 1. When your project is upgraded to Visual Basic.NET, most constants are changed automatically for you; however, if you use underlying values or variables instead of the constant names, many cases cannot be upgraded automatically. Using constant names minimizes the number of modifications you have to do.

Arrays and Fixed-Length Strings in User-Defined Types

Due to changes made which allow Visual Basic.NET arrays and structures to be fully compatible with other Visual Studio.NET languages, fixed-length strings are no longer supported in the language. In most cases this is not a problem, because there is a compatibility class which provides fixed-length string behavior, so the code:

```
Dim MyFixedLengthString As String * 100
```

upgrades to the following:

```
Dim MyFixedLengthString As New VB6.FixedLengthString(100)
```

However, fixed-length strings do cause a problem when used in structures (also known as user-defined types). The problem arises because the fixed-length string class is not automatically created when the user-defined type is created. An additional problem is that fixed-size arrays are not created, either, when the user-defined type is created.

When your code is upgraded, user-defined types with fixed-length strings or arrays will be marked with a comment telling you to initialize the fixed-length string or array before using the user-defined type. However, you can shield yourself from this modification by changing your Visual Basic 6.0 user-defined types to use strings instead of fixed-length strings, and uninitialized arrays instead of fixed-size arrays.

For example:

```
Private Type MyType
    MyArray(5) As Integer
    MyFixedString As String * 100
End Type
Sub Bar()
    Dim MyVariable As MyType
End Sub
```

can be changed to:

```
Private Type MyType
    MyArray() As Integer
    MyFixedString As String
End Type
Sub Bar()
    Dim MyVariable As MyType
    ReDim MyVariable.MyArray(5) As Integer
    MyVariable.MyFixedString = String$(100, " ")
End Sub
```

Avoid Legacy Features

Because they have been removed from the language, you should avoid using the following keywords:

- **Def<type>**
- **Computed GoTo/GoSub**
- **GoSub/Return**
- **Option Base 0|1**
- **VarPtr, ObjPtr, StrPtr**
- **LSet**

These are explained in more detail below.

Def<type>

In previous versions of Visual Basic, DefBool, DefByte, DefInt, DefLng, DefCur, DefSng, DefDbl, DefDec, DefDate, DefStr, DefObj and DefVar were used in the declarations section of a module to define a range of variables as a certain type. For example:

```
DefInt A-C
```

defined all variables beginning with the letter A, B, or C as an integer. Instead of using **Def<type>** statements, you should explicitly declare variables.

Computed GoTo/GoSub

Computed GoTo/GoSub statements take this form:

```
On x GoTo 100, 200, 300
```

These are not supported in Visual Basic.NET. Instead, you should use **If** statements, and Select Case constructs.

GoSub/Return

GoSub and **Return** statements are not supported in Visual Basic.NET. In most cases you can replace these with functions and procedures.

Option Base 0|1

Option Base 0|1 was used to specify the default lower bound of an array. As mentioned previously, this statement has been removed from the language since Visual Basic.NET natively only supports arrays with a zero lower bound. Non-zero lower bound arrays are supported through a wrapper class.

VarPtr, ObjPtr, StrPtr

VarPtr, **VarPrtArray**, **VarPtrStringArray**, **ObjPtr** and **StrPtr** were undocumented functions used to get the underlying memory address of variables. These functions are not supported in Visual Basic.NET.

LSet

In Visual Basic 6.0, the **LSet** statement could be used to assign a variable of one user-defined type to another variable of a different user-defined type. This functionality is not supported in Visual Basic.NET.

Windows APIs

Many APIs can be used exactly as they were in Visual Basic 6.0, with the caveat that you have to adjust your data types accordingly. The Visual Basic 6.0 **Long** datatype is now the Visual Basic.NET **Integer** datatype, and the Visual Basic 6.0 **Integer** datatype is now the Visual Basic.NET **Short** datatype. During the upgrade, these changes are made for you, and simple APIs work exactly the same as they did in Visual Basic 6.0. For example:

```
Private Declare Function GetVersion Lib "kernel32" () As Long
Function GetVer()
    Dim Ver As Long
    Ver = GetVersion()
    MsgBox ("System Version is " & Ver)
End Function
```

changes to:

```
Private Declare Function GetVersion Lib "kernel32" () As Integer
Function GetVer()
    Dim Ver As Integer
    Ver = GetVersion()
    MsgBox("System Version is " & Ver)
End Function
```

In addition to numeric datatype upgrades, Visual Basic 6.0 had a fixed-length string data type which is not supported in Visual Basic.NET, and which is upgraded to a fixed-length string wrapper class. In many cases in Visual Basic 6.0 you can perform the same action using a normal string. For example:

```
Private Declare Function GetUserName Lib "advapi32.dll" Alias _
"GetUserNameA" (ByVal lpBuffer As String, ByRef nSize As Long) As Long
Function GetUser()
    Dim Ret As Long
    Dim UserName As String
    Dim Buffer As String * 25
    Ret = GetUserName(Buffer, 25)
    UserName = Left$(Buffer, InStr(Buffer, Chr(0)) - 1)
    MsgBox (UserName)
End Function
```

can be better written using a normal string explicitly set to length 25 instead of a fixed-length string:

```
Dim Buffer As String
Buffer = String$(25, " ")
```

This is upgraded to Visual Basic.NET as follows:

```
Declare Function GetUserName Lib "advapi32.dll" Alias _
"GetUserNameA" (ByVal lpBuffer As String, ByRef nSize As Integer) As Integer
Function GetUser()
    Dim Ret As Integer
    Dim UserName As String
    Dim Buffer As String
    Buffer = New String(CChar(" "), 25)
    Ret = GetUserName(Buffer, 25)
    UserName = Left(Buffer, InStr(Buffer, Chr(0)) - 1)
    MsgBox(UserName)
End Function
```

In some cases, Visual Basic.NET better handles passing strings to APIs, since you can optionally declare how you want strings to be passed using the **ANSI** and **UNICODE** keywords.

There are three cases where you may need to make some changes. The first is passing user-defined types that contain fixed-length strings or byte arrays to APIs. In Visual Basic.NET you may need to change your code, adding the **MarshallAs** attribute (from **System.Runtime.InteropServices**) to each fixed-length string or byte array in the user-defined type. The second case is using the **As Any** variable type in a **Declare** statement. This is not supported in Visual Basic.NET. Variables of type **As Any** were often used to pass a variable that was either a string or Null; you can replace this Visual Basic 6.0 usage by declaring two forms of the API, one with longs, one with strings. For example, the GetPrivateProfileString API has a parameter *lpKeyName* of type **As Any**:

```
Private Declare Function GetPrivateProfileString Lib "kernel32" Alias
    "GetPrivateProfileStringA" (ByVal lpApplicationName As String, ByVal
        lpKeyName As Any, ByVal lpDefault As String, ByVal
            lpReturnedString As String, ByVal nSize As Long, ByVal
                lpFileName As String) As Long
```

You can remove the "As Any" by replacing the **Declare** with two versions; one that accepts a long, and one that accepts a string:

```
Private Declare Function GetPrivateProfileStringKey Lib "kernel32" Alias
    "GetPrivateProfileStringA" (ByVal lpApplicationName As String, ByVal
        lpKeyName As String, ByVal lpDefault As String, ByVal
            lpReturnedString As String, ByVal nSize As Long, ByVal
                lpFileName As String) As Long
Private Declare Function GetPrivateProfileStringNullKey Lib "kernel32"
    Alias "GetPrivateProfileStringA" (ByVal lpApplicationName As String,
        ByVal lpKeyName As Long, ByVal lpDefault As String, ByVal
            lpReturnedString As String, ByVal nSize As Long, ByVal
                lpFileName As String) As Long
```

When you wish to pass the value Null to the API, you use the **GetPrivateProfileStringNullKey** version. Doing it this way means that the function upgrades to Visual Basic.NET.

The final area where you may need to make some changes is if you are using APIs that perform thread creation, Windows subclassing, message queue hooking, and so on. Some of these functions will cause a run-time error in Visual Basic.NET. Many of these APIs have equivalents in Visual Basic.NET or the .NET Framework. You will have to fix these on a case-by-case basis.

Considerations for Forms and Controls

Visual Basic.NET has a new forms package, Windows Forms. Windows Forms is largely compatible with the forms package found in Visual Basic 6; however, there are some key differences that are outlined below:

- Windows Forms does not support the OLE container control; you should avoid using this control in your Visual Basic 6.0 applications.

- There is no shape control in Windows Forms. Square and rectangular shapes will be upgraded to labels, while ovals and circles cannot be upgraded. You should avoid using these in your applications.

- There is no line control in Windows Forms. Horizontal and vertical lines are upgraded to labels. Diagonal lines are not upgraded, and you should avoid using them.

- Windows Forms has a new set of graphics commands that replace the Form methods **Circle**, **CLS**, **PSet**, **Line**, and **Point**. Because the new object model is quite different from Visual Basic 6.0, these methods cannot be upgraded.

- For the Timer control, setting the **Interval** property to 0 does not disable the timer; instead the interval is reset to 1. In your Visual Basic 6.0 projects, you should set **Enabled** to **False** instead of setting the **Interval** to 0.

- Windows Forms has two menu controls, MainMenu and ContextMenu, whereas Visual Basic 6.0 has one menu control, Menu, which can be opened as a MainMenu or a ContextMenu. Menu controls are upgraded to MainMenu controls, but you will not be able to use them as ContextMenus; you will have to recreate your ContextMenus.

- Windows Forms has no support for Dynamic Data Exchange (DDE).

- Windows Forms does not support the **Form.PrintForm** method.

- Although Windows Forms has support for drag-and-drop functionality, the object model is quite different from Visual Basic 6.0. Therefore, the Visual Basic 6.0 drag-and-drop properties and methods cannot be upgraded.

- The .NET framework has an improved Clipboard object (**System.WinForms.Clipboard**) that offers more functionality and supports more clipboard formats than the Visual Basic 6.0 Clipboard object. However, because of differences between object models, clipboard statements cannot be automatically upgraded.

- Windows Forms does not support the **Name** property for forms and controls at run time; therefore you should not write code that iterates the **Controls** collection looking for a control with a certain name (this functionality is now available using the .NET **System.Reflection** classes.)

- To ensure your forms are upgraded to the right size, you should always use the default ScaleMode of twips in your applications. During the upgrade, Visual Basic.NET transforms your forms coordinates from twips to pixels.

- Windows Forms only supports true-type and open-type fonts. If your application uses other fonts, these fonts will be changed to the system's default font, and all formatting (size, bold, italic, underline) will be lost. This applies to the default VB6 font MS Sans Serif. For this reason, we recommend you use Arial instead of MS Sans Serif, wherever you have formatted text.

Visual Basic for the Microsoft .NET Framework

This article by Ted Pattison, an instructor and researcher at DevelopMentor, was published in the January 2001 issue of MSDN Magazine. Visual Basic.NET is the result of a substantial rebuild of Visual Basic for the Microsoft .NET Framework. There are several changes that make Visual Basic.NET easier to use and more powerful than Visual Basic 6.0 and that give it the kind of access to system resources that previously required the use of such languages as C++. One of the most important additions is object inheritance. In Visual Basic.NET, all managed types derive from System.Object. A significant new language feature is garbage collection, which is administered by the Common Language Runtime and provides improved memory management. The universal type system facilitates greater interoperability, also contributing to the enhanced power and flexibility found in Visual Basic.NET.

If you haven't done so already, it's time to get a handle on the Visual Basic.NET programming language. My goal in this article is to provide you with an introductory, yet intensive, look at Visual Basic.NET and the new Microsoft® .NET platform. In order to learn what Visual Basic.NET is all about, you must first understand a few core aspects of the .NET platform. This article will build your knowledge of Visual Basic.NET from the ground up, so I'll begin by discussing the new programming model and the high-level architecture of the platform's execution engine called the common language runtime (CLR).

While explaining what the CLR is and how it works, I'll show a few examples using Visual Basic.NET. As you'll see, Visual Basic® has undergone a significant overhaul to accommodate the CLR and its associated programming model. Consequently, Visual Basic.NET has many new object-oriented design features and much higher levels of type safety than previous versions of Visual Basic.

It is also important to know that Visual Basic.NET omits quite a few forms of syntax that were used in previous versions of Visual Basic. This means code written in Visual Basic 6.0 will not compile until you make a number of modifications. Furthermore, writing the best possible code in Visual Basic.NET usually involves using features and syntax that are not supported in Visual Basic 6.0. As a result, migrating Visual Basic 6.0 projects to Visual Basic.NET typically requires a rewrite rather than a simple port.

Migrating a Visual Basic 6.0 project to Visual Basic.NET could also involve significant rewriting due to dependencies on older libraries such as the Visual Basic for Applications (VBA) runtime or ActiveX® Data Objects (ADO). To become an effective .NET programmer, you should fully embrace the shared class libraries that are built into the CLR.

Visual Basic.NET is one of several new languages that have been designed specifically for the CLR and the .NET Framework. Another language that's getting a good deal of attention is C#. Like many other programmers using Visual Basic you're probably curious about how C# compares to Visual Basic.NET. Like Visual Basic.NET, C# is a language designed exclusively to target the CLR and the .NET platform. However, unlike Visual Basic.NET, C# has been designed to be especially friendly to programmers who are already proficient in C and C++. Throughout this article, I'll point out a few key differences that might lead you to prefer one of these languages over the other. However, I truly believe that either language can be used to write software that takes full advantage of the CLR and the .NET Framework. Now, let me get started by introducing the core concepts of the .NET platform.

The Role of the CLR

Code written for the .NET platform runs under the control of the CLR. It's important to note that the CLR has been architected to replace the existing runtime layers of COM, Microsoft Transaction Services (MTS), and COM+ (see the following table). As you can see, the CLR finally eliminates the need for a Visual Basic runtime layer.

	Windows NT 4.0	Windows 2000	.NET Platform
Your Code	Unmanaged Visual Basic 6.0 code	Unmanaged Visual Basic 6.0 code	Managed Visual Basic.NET code
Language-specific Integration Layer	Visual Basic Runtime MSVBVM60.DLL	Visual Basic Runtime MSVBVM60.DLL	CLR Runtime MSCOREE.DLL MSCORLIB.DLL
Context Concurrency Transactions	MTS Runtime MTXEX.DLL	COM+ Runtime OLE32.DLL OLEAUT32.DLL	CLR Runtime MSCOREE.DLL MSCORLIB.DLL
Class Loading and Remoting	COM Runtime OLE32.DLL OLEAUT32.DLL	COM+ RuntimeOLE32.DLL OLEAUT32.DLL	CLR Runtime MSCOREE.DLL MSCORLIB.DLL

Obviously, the CLR isn't going to replace COM overnight. Many companies have a considerable investment in code written for applications based on COM, MTS, and COM+. Therefore, interoperability between COM-based software and software written for the CLR will be an important issue. Microsoft has made a considerable investment to ensure that the CLR-to-COM interoperability layer works as smoothly and efficiently as possible. However, it should be clear that in the long term, Microsoft expects the majority of development for Windows to move to the CLR and the .NET platform.

Code written to run exclusively under the control of the CLR is called managed code. Older code that relies on COM and the Win32® API is known as unmanaged code. Visual Basic 6.0 is only capable of producing unmanaged code, while Visual Basic.NET is only capable of producing managed code. Herein lies a fundamental difference between these two versions of Visual Basic.

The Visual Basic team has created a new version of the Visual Basic compiler (VBC.EXE) for producing managed executables (DLLs and EXEs). For example, you can build a managed DLL by feeding one or more Visual Basic source code files to the Visual Basic.NET compiler. Note that, unlike previous versions of Visual Basic, by convention Visual Basic.NET source code files have a .VB extension. While it makes writing and compiling Visual Basic source code much easier, Visual Studio.NET is not a requirement for writing software with Visual Basic.NET. You can write Visual Basic.NET source code in any editor, then build your DLLs and EXEs from the command line.

Visual Basic.NET eases the management of source code because you can maintain all the code for an entire project in a single source file. Unlike earlier versions of Visual Basic, you don't have to define each class in a separate .CLS file. You do, of course, have the flexibility to maintain the code for a single project in many .VB files and compile them into a single binary for distribution.

Another nice new feature is that Visual Basic.NET makes it possible to automate production builds using the NMAKE.EXE utility and a MAKEFILE. Companies that maintain lots of separate source files and are continually compiling test and production builds will see this as an improvement over Visual Basic 6.0.

Managed Types

Let's look at what it takes to write and compile a simple console-based application with Visual Basic.NET. As you look at the code in Example 1, keep in mind that code written for the CLR is based on the notion of managed types. This example contains two managed type definitions: MyApp and Class1.

Example 1. Console-based App Using Visual Basic.NET

```
' in the source file Hello.vb
Module MyApp
  Sub Main()
    Dim obj As Class1 = New Class1
    System.Console.WriteLine(obj.Method1)
  End Sub
End Module


Class Class1
  Function Method1()As String
    Return "Hello Visual Basic.NET"
  End Function
End Class
```

The MyApp module contains a single method named Main, which represents the entry point for this console application. The implementation of the Main method creates an instance of Class1 and calls Method1. The return value of Method1 is used to write a message to the console window. This example demonstrates a new syntactic convenience provided by Visual Basic.NET. You can now declare and initialize a variable in a single line of code.

The other managed type definition in Example 1 is Class1. This class contains a single method named Method1. Method1 also includes a new convenience provided by Visual Basic.NET: it uses the Return statement to pass its return value back to the caller. With Visual Basic.NET it's no longer necessary to assign return values using the name of the function.

Finally, take a look at the syntax in Example 1 for accessing the Console class from the CLR class libraries. Note that the code that calls the WriteLine method on the Console class is qualified with the word System. In this case, System is being used as a namespace. The concept of namespaces is very important to the CLR and, therefore, to Visual Basic.NET. You must understand how namespaces work when you need to resolve the names of managed types from other libraries.

A namespace is a user-defined scope in which managed types are defined. Most of the CLR built-in types are defined within the System namespace, such as System.Object, System.Int32, and System.String. Note that a namespace can be nested within another namespace, as in the case of System.Data, which holds classes such as System.Data.DataSet.

Visual Basic.NET provides a syntactic shortcut via the Imports statement when programming against types declared within a namespace. For example, suppose you add this line to the top of your Visual Basic.NET source file:

```
Imports System
```

This Imports statement makes it possible to call the WriteLine method without full qualification, as shown here:

```
Console.WriteLine ' this can be used
System.Console.WriteLine ' instead of this
```

Note that the using statement in C# provides identical support to the Visual Basic.NET Imports statement. You should also understand that the Imports statement does nothing more than make your statements more concise when typing in the names of other managed types.

Using the Visual Basic.NET Compiler

You can compile the source code from Example 1 into a console application EXE by running the following command from the command line:

```
vbc.exe /target:exe hello.vb
```

While the code in this example is very simple, it allows me to illustrate some key aspects of developing software for the .NET platform. When you've successfully built a project with the Visual Basic.NET compiler, you have created a binary that holds one or more managed type definitions. These managed types are then ready to be loaded and run under the control of the CLR.

The programming model of the CLR recognizes four primary kinds of managed types: classes, interfaces, structures, and enumerations. Example 2 shows what each one looks like in Visual Basic.NET.

Example 2. Managed Types

```
Enum Enum1
  Value1
  Value2
End Enum

Structure Structure1
  Public Field1 As Integer
  Public Field2 As Long
End Structure

Interface Interface1
  Sub Method1()
  Sub Method2()
End Interface

Class Class1
      Implements Interface1
  Public Field1 As Integer
  Private Field2 As Long
  Sub Method1() Implements Interface1.Method1
    ' implementation
  End Sub
  Sub Method2() Implements Interface1.Method2
    ' implementation
  End Sub
  Shared Sub Method3()
    ' implementation
  End Sub
End Class
```

Unlike previous versions of Visual Basic, Visual Basic.NET does not support user-defined types (UDTs) or the Type keyword. UDTs have been replaced with the structure type. A structure type is similar to a UDT in that it is a value type; it can be allocated on the stack or wholly embedded inside another type. Structures are a valuable alternative to classes because they can provide a more efficient way to store and pass data. It's also important to note that structure types are more versatile than UDTs were because structures can expose public methods and even implement an interface. You should think of a structure as a managed type used to create lightweight objects.

Both the CLR and Visual Basic.NET have excellent support for interface-based programming. Unlike Visual Basic 6.0, you no longer have to fudge an interface definition using a class construct. Example 2 shows the basic syntax for defining an interface and implementing it in a class. From this simple example, you should be able to see that the syntax for interface-based programming is far more elegant than the syntax in Visual Basic 6.0.

Shared members is another critical concept of the CLR programming model that will be new to many programmers experienced with Visual Basic. For example, a class can contain shared methods and shared fields, in addition to instance methods and instance fields. This is very different from Visual Basic 6.0, where classes could only contain instance members.

A shared member differs from an instance member in that it can be accessed without creating an instance from the class. Let's look at a simple example from Example 2. Examine Method3 in Class1, which has been marked as a shared method. Note that the keyword Shared in Visual Basic.NET has the same meaning as the static keyword in languages such as C#, C++, and Java.

A client can access a shared method simply by calling the shared method name together with the class name, like this:

```
Class1.Method3
```

Another interesting thing to note is that the programming model of the CLR has no direct mapping to the Visual Basic.NET Module type. The Visual Basic.NET programming language includes the Module type largely to provide an equivalent to .BAS modules in older versions of Visual Basic. However, when you build a DLL or an .EXE, the Visual Basic.NET compiler silently transforms each module type in your source code into a managed class that can be loaded and run by the CLR.

You should think of a module as a special class type that cannot be used to create objects. It can contain only shared members; it cannot contain instance members. You have to keep on your toes, because although every member of a module is implicitly shared, you'll experience a compile-time error if you add the Shared keyword to any one.

Last, you should note that a module type offers one syntactic convenience over the class type in Visual Basic.NET: you can call a shared method defined in a module without using the module name. When you call a shared method from a class, you must do so using the class name, or alternatively add an Imports statement with the class name.

The programming model of the CLR also includes a few other familiar abstractions. Classes and structures use fields for defining typed units of storage and use methods to provide behavior. The CLR also recognizes properties. As you know from earlier versions of Visual Basic, a property is a method (or a set of methods) that appears to the client as an exposed field. While the syntax for declaring properties changes between Visual Basic 6.0 and Visual Basic.NET, the motivations for using them are exactly the same. The key point here is that the abstraction of properties is recognized by the underlying programming model of the CLR.

You should note that the CLR, like COM and Visual Basic 6.0, supports indexed properties. As a result, you will, from time to time, see client code that looks like this:

```
Dim s As String
s = Object1.Property1(10)
```

An indexed property can also be assigned as a default property for a class. (C# uses the term "indexer" to refer to an indexed property that's been marked as default.) Here's an example of what client code looks like when accessing a default indexed property:

```
Dim s As String
s = Object1(10)
```

Note that a property cannot be marked as the default for a class unless it is indexed. This is a big change from earlier versions of Visual Basic. Here's an example of Visual Basic 6.0 code that retrieves a non-indexed default property from a textbox:

```
Dim var1 As Variant
var1 = frmMain.txtCustomer
```

Earlier versions of Visual Basic suffer from an awkward ambiguity caused by the inclusion of non-indexed default properties. How does that Visual Basic compiler know whether you intend to assign the default property of the textbox or a reference to the actual textbox object?

The classic way to solve this ambiguity in Visual Basic has been to use the Set keyword to distinguish the assignment of a object reference from the assignment of the object's default property value. For example, if you want to assign a reference to the textbox object instead of its default property value, you write the following code:

```
Dim var1 As Variant
Set var1 = frmMain.txtCustomer
```

As you have just seen, earlier versions of Visual Basic require the Set keyword due to the ambiguities caused by non-indexed default properties. Since Visual Basic.NET eliminates non-indexed default properties, the Set keyword is no longer needed. In fact, Visual Basic.NET does not support the Set keyword for assignment operations. This means you'll experience a compilation error if you use the Set keyword when assigning an object reference. You have to admit, that's a pretty big syntactic change when migrating from Visual Basic 6.0 to Visual Basic.NET.

Delegates and Events

The delegate is a new concept that's central to the programming model of the CLR. A delegate is a special type of managed class that allows you to work with type-safe function pointers. Each delegate type is based on a single method signature. When you create an instance of a delegate, you must provide the address of a method implementation with a matching signature. Once you've created the delegate instance, it's pretty simple to invoke the method.

Example 3 demonstrates the most fundamental Visual Basic.NET syntax required to declare and use a delegate. Note the use of the keywords Delegate and AddressOf. You should also see from this example that there is a longhand syntax and a more concise shorthand syntax, both of which produce the same results. Once you understand what delegates are and how they work, you can appreciate how the CLR uses them to provide sophisticated support for more advanced features, such as multicasting and events.

Example 3. Delegate Example

```
Delegate Sub Delegate1(ByVal s As String)

Module MyApp

  Sub Sub1(ByVal s As String)
    System.Console.WriteLine("From Sub1: " & s)
  End Sub

  Sub Sub2(ByVal s As String)
    System.Console.WriteLine("From Sub2: " & s)
  End Sub

  Sub Main
    Dim MyFunctionPointer As Delegate1
    ' longhand syntax for creating and using a delegate
    MyFunctionPointer = New Delegate1(AddressOf Sub1)
    MyFunctionPointer.Invoke("Test message 1")
    ' shorthand syntax for creating and using a delegate
    MyFunctionPointer = AddressOf Sub2
```

```
    MyFunctionPointer("Test message 2")
  End Sub

End Module
```

A multicast delegate is like a collection of function pointers that facilitates the execution of a set of method implementations using a single line of code. Whenever you create a delegate using the Delegate keyword, remember that the Visual Basic.NET compiler creates a multicast delegate as opposed to a simple delegate. This gives you the ability to hook up multiple method implementations to a single delegate.

The following code shows a variation on the delegate example shown in Example 3.

```
Dim d1, d2, d3 As Delegate1
d1 = AddressOf Sub1
d2 = AddressOf Sub2
' create d3 which is a multicast of d1 and d2
d3 = CType(System.Delegate.Combine(d1, d2), Delegate1)
d3("Firing two method implementations at once")
```

A third delegate, d3, is created as a combination of the other two. The last line of code in this example executes the method implementations for both Sub1 and Sub2. While this example uses a multicast delegate to fire two implementations, you can hook up and execute as many method implementations as you'd like. The CLR worries about the plumbing details of actually invoking the calls. You just have to make sure that the delegate and all the methods share a common signature.

Now that you understand the basic idea of a multicast delegate, you can begin to appreciate how the CLR supports events on a managed class. The CLR event architecture is based on the idea of a source object using multicast delegates to execute method implementations on one or more listener objects.

As is the case in Visual Basic 6.0, a Visual Basic.NET class can contain events in addition to methods, fields, and properties. Example 4 shows the basic code required to register two listener classes with an event source class. In Visual Basic.NET, the way events work is similar to how they work in Visual Basic 6.0, as far as syntax is concerned. For example, Visual Basic.NET provides familiar keywords such as Event, RaiseEvent, and WithEvents. Visual Basic.NET also introduces the Handles keyword for creating listenermethods.

Example 4. A Visual Basic.NET Class

```
Public Class EventClass1
  Public Event OnEvent1()
  Public Sub Method1()
    RaiseEvent OnEvent1()
  End Sub
End Class
```

(continued)

(continued)

```
Class ListenerClass1
  Private WithEvents Source As EventClass1
  Public Sub Register(ByVal s As EventClass1)
    Source = s
  End Sub
  Public Sub Unregister()
    Source = Nothing
  End Sub
  Private Sub TedsHandler() Handles Source.OnEvent1
    System.Console.WriteLine("Listener 1 handler executing")
  End Sub
End Class

Class ListenerClass2
  Private WithEvents Source As EventClass1
  Public Sub Register(ByVal s As EventClass1)
    Source = s
  End Sub
  Public Sub Unregister()
    source = Nothing
  End Sub
  Private Sub FredsHandler() Handles Source.OnEvent1
    System.Console.WriteLine("Listener 2 handler executing")
  End Sub
End Class

Module MyApp
  Public Sub Main()
    ' create event source object
    Dim ec As EventClass1 = New EventClass1
    ' create and sink up listener 1 object
    Dim listener1 As ListenerClass1 = New ListenerClass1
    listener1.Register(ec)
    ' create and sink up listener 2 object
    Dim listener2 As ListenerClass2 = New ListenerClass2
    listener2.Register(ec)
    ' call method which triggers events
    ec.Method1()
  End Sub
End Module
```

While the syntax for programming events remains largely the same, the plumbing used down below has completely changed from that of Visual Basic 6.0. Events in earlier versions of Visual Basic are based on COM and the ConnectionPoint interfaces. As I've mentioned, events in the CLR are based upon multicast delegates. A class that contains events can be used to create an event source object, which sends notifications to listener objects.

The use of keywords such as Event, RaiseEvent, WithEvents, and Handles instructs the Visual Basic.NET compiler to emit lots of extra code to deal with delegate registration behind the scenes. That means you don't have to work with delegates directly when raising or listening for events. Note that much of this extra productivity is specific to Visual Basic.NET and is not included in other managed languages, such as C#.

I've just taken a brief look at the different kinds of managed types that make up the programming model of the CLR. Now that I've covered some of the basics, let's take a more in-depth look at what gets compiled into a managed executable.

Microsoft Intermediate Language and JIT Compilation

TheCLR, as its name implies, was designed to allow for an unprecedented level of integration between all languages that target the .NET platform. This means that the Visual Basic.NET compiler, along with the compilers of other managed languages, such as C#, must follow the same set of rules. One of the most important rules is that executable instructions must be compiled into DLLs and EXEs in the form of Microsoft Intermediate Language (MSIL).

MSIL is a compiled format that is both similar to and very different from traditional assembly code. It is similar to assembly code in that it contains low-level instructions where things are being pushed, popped, and moved in and out of registers. However, it is very different in that it contains no dependencies on any particular operating system and hardware platform. This means that after an EXE or DLL containing MSIL is deployed on a target computer, it must still undergo a final round of just-in-time (JIT) compilation to transform it into machine-specific assembly instructions.

The first key benefit to MSIL is that it allows the CLR to verify during JIT compilation that the managed code is completely type safe. The CLR relies on this verification process to ensure that code distributed inside a DLL or EXE doesn't play tricks with pointers or illegal type conversions. This allows the CLR to protect itself from many commonly used system attacks. A computer that downloads managed code from an untrusted source can protect itself in a way that unmanaged code can't.

A second obvious benefit of MSIL is that it decouples your EXEs and DLLs from any specific operating system or hardware platform. Microsoft currently has plans to ship a version of the CLR for Windows 2000, Windows NT®, Windows 98, and Windows 95. However, MSIL is powerful because it gives your DLLs and EXEs the potential of running on platforms other than those based on the Intel *x86* processors.

You are likely to see a version of the CLR for Windows CE in the near future. It is also entirely possible that you will see implementations of the CLR built for other operating systems and hardware platforms as well. The idea of running your Visual Basic code on a hardware platform such as a handheld device or Pocket PC is a reality today.

The CLR as a Better COM

While you might be somewhat apprehensive about Microsoft's long-term decision to replace COM with the CLR, you should strive to understand the underlying advantages of migrating from the old runtime environment to the new one. The architects that designed the CLR and the .NET platform were able to incorporate the best aspects of COM while alleviating much of the pain of writing and deploying COM-based applications.

In particular, the CLR has eliminated many of COM's most frustrating problems with regard to language interoperability, application deployment, and component versioning. As you might have guessed, the new programming model introduced by the CLR serves to eliminate many of COM's unnecessarily confusing details with regard to writing and understanding the code for a distributed application.

The history of COM has been plagued with problems concerning interoperability of various languages. While a certain degree of interoperability exists between unmanaged languages, it is far from ideal. For example, it's common for C++ programmers to produce component DLLs that are unusable from Visual Basic or scripting languages. Many built-in C++ types for dealing with things such as strings, arrays, and pointers are either impossible or impractical to consume from other languages.

The CLR ensures higher levels of interoperability. The programming model of the CLR is based on the universal type system shown in Figure 1. Every managed language must be layered on top of and mapped to this core set of built-in types.

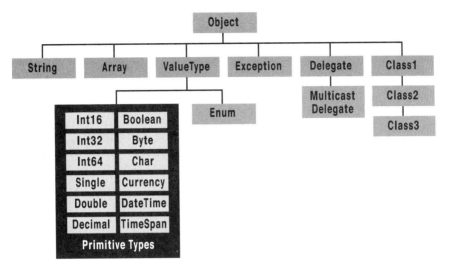

Figure 1. Universal Type System

As you can see in Figure 1, the CLR type system defines a predictable set of primitive types containing things like integers and floating point numbers. The CLR's type system also defines standard classes for other types, such as String, Array, and Exception.

Languages such as Visual Basic.NET and C# provide keywords that map directly to many of the built-in CLR types. For example, Visual Basic.NET provides the Integer keyword, which is the equivalent of the int keyword in C#. Both types map directly to the CLR's System.Int32 type. As you can see, the CLR improves upon COM by standardizing on a universal set of types that are shared across all managed languages.

You should know that the CLR provides a few types and features that are not supported by every managed language. For example, the CLR's type system provides various built-in types for unsigned integers. Unsigned integers are fully supported by C#, but not by Visual Basic.NET. This means there's a potential for a C# programmer to create a component that exposes unsigned integers in a manner that would make it either awkward or impossible to access from other languages.

In order to prevent situations in which programmers mistakenly create components that are inaccessible from other managed languages, Microsoft has created a document called the Common Language Specification (CLS). The CLS defines a subset of CLR types and features that component and consumer languages must support to effectively interoperate with other managed languages.

Visual Basic.NET is fully compliant with the CLS. In addition, the class libraries built into the CLR are fully accessible from any CLS-compliant language, including Visual Basic.NET. This is a great news for programmers using Visual Basic who, in the past, have had to accept that many parts of their underlying platform (such as the Win32 API and OLE32.DLL) are inaccessible from their chosen language. Full access to the CLR class libraries really levels the playing field with respect to what can be done with Visual Basic when compared to other managed languages.

As you can see from Figure 1, the type system of the CLR relies heavily on inheritance. The entire type system is based on a single-inheritance hierarchy. All managed types used to create objects ultimately derive from the single root type System.Object. When you create a class without explicitly inheriting from another class, your class implicitly inherits from System.Object. That means that a class declaration like this:

```
Public Class Class1
  ' class member declarations go here
End Class
```

is equivalent to this class declaration:

```
Public Class Class1
      Inherits System.Object
  ' class member declarations go here
End Class
```

If you want to derive one user-defined class from another, the syntax looks like this:

```
Public Class Class2
      Inherits Class1
  ' class member declarations go here
End Class
```

Note that Visual Basic.NET requires you to separate the name of the deriving class and the Inherits keyword using a line break. If you'd like to write Visual Basic.NET code to purposely confuse all those know-it-all C++ programmers out there, you can substitute a colon for the line break like this:

```
Public Class Class2 : Inherits Class1
  ' class member declarations go here
End Class
```

This syntax more closely resembles C# and C++, where the colon is required when using inheritance. However, with Visual Basic.NET, it's important to realize that the colon is just acting as a line break. I have actually gotten hooked on this style because I find it more manageable and more readable. OK, and yes, I use it because I've always been a C++ wannabe.

A key point to observe is that any managed type from which you can create an instance ultimately inherits from System.Object. This also includes primitive types such as integers, longs, and doubles. This means that all variables can be cast to the System.Object type regardless of whether they are reference types or value types. You should also keep in mind that the Visual Basic.NET language has moved the functionality of older unmanaged types such as the variant, IUnknown and IDispatch into System.Object.

A Richer Format for Component Metadata

The .NET Framework uses the term "module" to refer to a managed binary such as a DLL or an EXE. Every managed language must have a compiler that is capable of building an extensive set of component metadata into each module to describe the types it contains. As you can see from Figure 2, a module holds component metadata and the MSIL code for the managed types it contains.

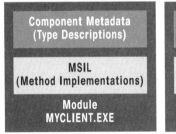

Figure 2. A .NET Module

The component metadata in a module is similar to the type information stored in the type library of a COM DLL because it exposes information to client applications about its public types (such as enumerations, structures, interfaces, and classes). However, there are a few important differences that make the type information for managed components much richer than the type information used by COM.

First, all component metadata must adhere to a single, high-fidelity format for describing managed type information. This eliminates problems experienced by COM developers with fidelity loss between the type information format used in type libraries and the format used in Interface Definition Language (IDL). What's more, .NET development is easier than COM development because you never need a separate language like IDL to define your types. Custom types can always be fully described using a managed language such as Visual Basic.NET or C#.

Another big difference between COM and the CLR is that managed components contain far more metadata for describing classes. In COM, a class's type information is defined in a type library in terms of a coclass. The COM coclass type is limited in the sense that it only describes a class in terms of which interfaces it supports. COM has very strict rules about separating interface from implementation, and the limited information in a coclasses definition is very much in line with that philosophy.

While COM requires a formal separation of interface from implementation, Visual Basic has always made things easier by automatically building a default interface behind every multiuse class. When a Visual Basic client contains a reference variable based on a class name, the Visual Basic compiler silently casts the reference to the default interface for the class. Visual Basic, therefore, has been able to hide the fact that COM requires a formal separation of interface from implementation types.

The architects of the CLR have taken a view of classes that is much more in line with Visual Basic than with COM. The component metadata for a managed class can expose its public methods as part of a default interface. This offers much more flexibility. Unlike COM, you don't need to define a standalone interface in order to program against a class. The key point is that you don't have to work in terms of interfaces in situations when a class with public methods is an acceptable and much easier alternative.

While the CLR architects have removed the requirement to work in terms of standalone interfaces, you should by no means interpret this to mean that interface-based programming isn't important when writing managed code. Programming in terms of explicit interfaces is as important as ever when you want to create plug-compatible classes or decouple one subsystem from another in a large scale application. Furthermore, the CLR class libraries frequently expose their functionality through interfaces. Any intermediate or advanced programmer should be very comfortable defining, implementing, and using interface types.

While both COM and the CLR require components to expose public type information, the CLR is different from COM in that it requires modules to expose internal type information to the system. This internal type information is used by the CLR at runtime to create and manage objects. This allows the CLR to perform many tasks which the COM runtime delegates to component DLLs and client applications. Let's look at an example.

A COM type library doesn't contain any type information to describe how objects should be represented in memory. Instead, it's the responsibility of a COM DLL to allocate and release the memory for its objects. A COM DLL also has the responsibility of laying out its objects with COM-compliant vtables. In the CLR, these responsibilities have been removed from component DLLs and transferred to the underlying runtime environment.

The CLR takes on the responsibility of allocating and releasing the memory for objects. When a client makes a request to create an object from a managed class, the CLR discovers the object's memory and layout requirements by examining internal type information about the class at runtime. This allows the CLR to allocate the proper amount of memory during object creation.

The CLR also uses internal type information to create the binding that allows clients to execute methods on objects. This means that managed binaries, unlike COM binaries, don't have to contain code to generate or access COM-style vtables.

As you can see, the CLR takes on more responsibilities than the COM runtime. This has allowed the CLR architects to remove much of the complexity and extra baggage that is built into COM binaries, such as class factories and code for dealing with vtables.

Garbage Collection for Managing Object Lifetimes

Now that I'm on the subject of memory management, I'd like to point out an important architectural difference between COM and the CLR. It has to do with the management of object lifetimes and has a dramatic effect on the way you should write your code.

COM uses reference counting to manage object lifetimes. When you release the last reference to a COM object, it synchronously removes itself from memory. If your class contains some custom cleanup code in an implementation of Class_Terminate, you get the guarantee that this code will run in a deterministic fashion. This is not the case when running managed objects in the CLR.

The CLR manages object lifetime through garbage collection. This is very different from the reference counting that COM uses to manage object lifetimes. The CLR always creates objects on a garbage-collected heap. When a client releases the last reference to an object, the object is not instantly removed from memory. Instead, the garbage collector removes the object from memory at some indeterminate time in the future.

The two primary reasons you would prefer garbage collection over reference counting are enhanced performance and the ability of the system to detect and break down circular references between objects. The designers of the CLR decided that these reasons were sufficient grounds for using garbage collection for lifetime management rather than using the model used by COM.

The primary reason some prefer reference counting over garbage collection is that your destructor (Class_Terminate) will fire in a timely and predictable manner. Since the CLR doesn't use reference counting, Visual Basic.NET does not support Class_Terminate. Instead, a managed class can provide a Finalize method that will fire when the object is removed from memory. However, it should be clear that things are much different from COM where the destructor for a class fires the instant the client releases it.

The debate about which is superior—garbage collection or reference counting—rages on. This debate has turned into a bit of a crusade for many developers. While I'll refrain from commenting on which style of lifetime management is better, I can safely say that the CLR uses garbage collection, and that fact should affect the way you write your managed code.

Assemblies and Code Distribution

As I mentioned earlier, a module is a binary unit of code which holds both component metadata and MSIL. However, there is another layer of abstraction for distributing managed code called an assembly. It complements the module because it addresses several important issues related to deployment, versioning, and security.

There are many important details concerning how assemblies are used to deploy managed code. Unfortunately, there are far too many details for me to cover in this article. I'll only scratch the surface, providing a high-level overview of the significant points.

An assembly can be defined as one or more modules that make up a unit of deployment. Each assembly contains a catalog of component metadata known as a manifest. The abstraction of the assembly is important because its manifest holds critical metadata about type visibility, component versioning, and security.

Every managed type must exist within the scope of an assembly. In Visual Basic.NET, each project you create will typically represent a single assembly. When you want to use managed types in your project from another assembly, your project must include a reference to this other assembly.

When you are creating an assembly for others to use, you should decide which types should be visible from outside the assembly. The keywords Public and Private allow you to expose or hide a type such as a class or interface. Note that Visual Basic.NET allows you to adorn methods in a public class using the Friend keyword, making the method accessible only from within the assembly.

One way to think of an assembly is that it is a unit of versioning. Your decision to make each type public or private is very important. Remember, you only need to consider versioning issues for types and type members that you have exposed to external clients. Types that are private to an assembly can be removed or modified without concern for existing client applications.

When you're calling VBC.EXE from the command line, you must pass a switch (/reference or /r) for each external assembly your project is using. For example, here's what a call to the Visual Basic.NET complier looks like when a console application is using types from a external assembly:

```
vbc.exe /target:exe /reference:MyLibrary.dll hello.vb
```

One assembly you never need to reference explicitly is MSCORLIB.DLL. Since this assembly contains the core managed types, such as System.Object, used by every project, the Visual Basic.NET compiler automatically includes a reference to it whether you add one or not. Other assemblies must be explicitly referenced, or your code will not compile. Note that Visual Studio.NET passes the appropriate arguments to the Visual Basic.NET compiler when you create references in your project.

In many cases, an assembly will consist of a single DLL or a single EXE file. By default, every DLL or EXE you build with the Visual Basic.NET compiler is both a module and an assembly. However, in a more complicated deployment scenario you might want to create an assembly that contains multiple DLLs and various resource files. There is a command-line switch for the Visual Basic.NET compiler that allows you to build a module that is not an assembly. This makes it possible to build multi-module assemblies using the assembly linker utility (AL.EXE).

The CLR recognizes two types of assemblies. The first, a private assembly, is deployed with and used by a single application. Note that a private assembly must be deployed in the same directory or in a subdirectory of the application that uses it. The second, a shared assembly, can be used by multiple applications. A shared assembly must be installed in a special assembly cache before it can be used by client applications.

Figures 3 and 4 provide high-level views of assemblies. Figure 3 shows a private assembly that consists of a single DLL. Figure 4 shows a more complex example of a shared assembly based on three different DLLs.

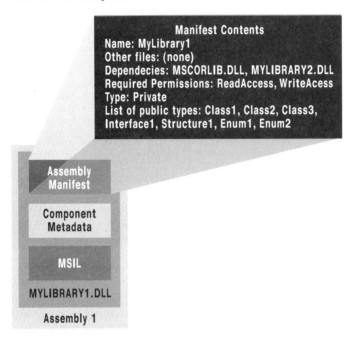

Figure 3. Private Assembly with One DLL

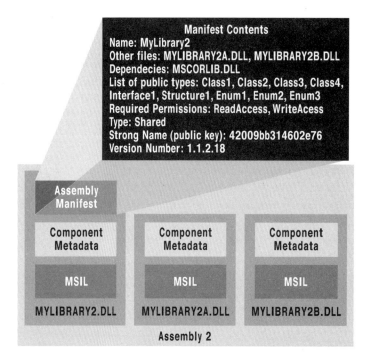

Figure 4. Shared Assembly

The End of DLL Hell

The CLR offers many advantages over COM when it comes to application deployment and component versioning. For example, COM has gained a reputation for being fragile and hard to deploy because it requires registry entries for things like ProgIDs, CLSIDs, IIDs, and type libraries. The CLR does not require similar registry entries for assemblies or managed types. The CLR provides much more flexibility and adaptability when it comes to finding loadable modules and resolving types at runtime.

The CLR also offers significant improvements over COM with respect to component versioning. This is largely due to the CLR's support for side-by-side deployment—in other words, the CLR's ability to load and work with multiple versions of the same assembly. The CLR makes it possible for two different applications to load and use two different versions of the same DLL even when they're running together inside the same process.

Side-by-side deployment is a great improvement over COM where a class (a CLSID) can only be deployed once per machine. This means it's now far more acceptable to create new versions of DLLs that do not maintain backwards compatibility with earlier versions. You can simply deploy multiple versions of a DLL in order to satisfy both new clients and old clients alike. Gone are the days when installing a new version of a DLL steps on an older version, breaking an existing client application.

The CLR provides sophisticated versioning support. However, it's important to know that this support is only available when you deploy your code in a shared assembly. I'll give you a brief description of how things work so you can appreciate why things are so much better than they are with COM versioning.

When you compile a client application that references a shared assembly, the assembly's name and version number are recorded in the client assembly's manifest. Unlike COM, a client application always knows which version of a DLL it was compiled against. Furthermore, the CLR makes it possible for a developer or an administrator to adjust the versioning policy for a client application to determine which version of a shared assembly gets loaded. A client application can be configured to load the exact version that it was compiled against or it can be configured to load the most recent, compatible version.

From this brief discussion of assemblies, you should be able to tell that the CLR provides a much improved environment for deploying applications and versioning components. You've probably heard many people at Microsoft touting this as the end of DLL Hell. From my perspective, this is one of the most tangible benefits of migrating applications to the CLR and Visual Basic.NET.

Visual Basic 6.0 to Visual Basic.NET Migration

As you can see, there are countless design issues and implementation details to consider when deciding whether to migrate from Visual Basic 6.0 and COM over to Visual Basic.NET and the CLR. Migrating will have its fair share of costs and benefits. You should also consider the differences between migrating a development team as opposed to migrating an existing Visual Basic 6.0 project.

Keep in mind that the programming model of the CLR supports many new object-oriented features in Visual Basic that will be new to developers. There are far more new programming features and concepts than I could possibly cover in this article. For starters, Visual Basic.NET includes support for structured error handling, shared class members, parameterized constructors, method overloading, and implementation inheritance.

Make no mistake about what it will take to migrate the average programmer from Visual Basic 6.0 to Visual Basic.NET. All these new object-oriented features are going to take time to master. There's a great deal to learn in order to use all these new features properly.

Keep in mind that migrating to Visual Basic.NET is not just about changing the way you write your syntax. You are also encouraged to use the built-in class libraries of the CLR whenever possible. These class libraries provide a wide range of functionality in areas such as string manipulation, user interface construction, database access, XML processing, and sockets programming.

Embracing the class libraries of the CLR requires a fundamental shift for programmers whose experience is with Visual Basic. When you need to manipulate text, you will be tempted to use familiar functions such as UCase, InStr, and StrComp from the VBA runtime library. However, you should resist this temptation and seek out the equivalent functionality from the CLR class libraries. As you can imagine, migrating programmers from existing libraries such as the VBA runtime, ADO, and MSXML to similar functionality in the CLR class libraries will have its associated costs.

Once you're up to speed with the new features of Visual Basic.NET and start to get comfortable with the CLR class libraries, I think you'll agree that they provide a much better platform for building distributed applications than anything you've ever used before. When you reach this point, I can say with confidence that you'll be very excited about using Visual Basic.NET whenever you start a new project.

However, it's not so easy to decide whether your current Visual Basic 6.0 project should be migrated over to Visual Basic.NET. Porting any project from Visual Basic 6.0 to Visual Basic.NET will be a nontrivial undertaking. Migrating an application or component library will require redesigning existing types and rewriting existing method implementations. Eliminating references to unmanaged libraries and replacing them with references to the CLR class libraries obviously makes migration all the more costly.

Some companies will come to the conclusion that it's simply not worth trying to port their existing Visual Basic 6.0 projects over to Visual Basic.NET. At this point, you have two options. You can rewrite the project from scratch in Visual Basic.NET or you can simply leave the project as it is in Visual Basic 6.0. If you decide to leave some of your applications and component libraries in Visual Basic 6.0, you'll be happy to discover that the CLR-to-COM interoperability layer is reliable and fairly easy to use.

The CLR-to-COM interoperability layer gives you the opportunity to build applications using a mix of managed and unmanaged code. This means you can mix and match Visual Basic.NET code with Visual Basic 6.0 code. I plan to cover many of these issues in far more depth in an upcoming Basic Instincts column.

Conclusion

There is no way you can understand what Visual Basic.NET is all about until you have a firm grasp of the CLR and its associated programming model. It's important that you learn about the underlying type system and object-oriented features of the CLR. Once you have learned these basics, you will be able to master a managed language such as Visual Basic.NET or C#.

Throughout this article I have described how many of the implementation details of COM have been replaced with newer, more modern implementations in the CLR. However, the spirit of COM is still very much alive in the CLR and the .NET Framework. It's all about writing, reusing, deploying, and versioning application code based on components. If it helps, you can simply think of the CLR as the most recent version of COM.

C# Introduction and Overview

This article was published in 2000 on MSDN Online. C# is a modern object-oriented language that enables programmers to quickly and easily build a wide range of applications for the new Microsoft .NET platform. The framework provided allows C# components to become Web services that are available across the Internet, from any application running on any platform. The language enhances developer productivity while serving to eliminate programming errors that can result in increased development costs. C# brings rapid Web development to the C and C++ programmer while maintaining the power and flexibility that those developers call for.

For the past two decades, C and C++ have been the most widely used languages for developing commercial and business software. While both languages provide the programmer with a tremendous amount of fine-grained control, this flexibility comes at a cost to productivity. Compared with a language such as Microsoft® Visual Basic®, equivalent C and C++ applications often take longer to develop. Due to the complexity and long cycle times associated with these languages, many C and C++ programmers have been searching for a language offering better balance between power and productivity.

There are languages today that raise productivity by sacrificing the flexibility that C and C++ programmers often require. Such solutions constrain the developer too much (for example, by omitting a mechanism for low-level code control) and provide least-common-denominator capabilities. They don't easily interoperate with preexisting systems, and they don't always mesh well with current Web programming practices.

The ideal solution for C and C++ programmers would be rapid development combined with the power to access all the functionality of the underlying platform. They want an environment that is completely in sync with emerging Web standards and one that provides easy integration with existing applications. Additionally, C and C++ developers would like the ability to code at a low level when and if the need arises.

Microsoft Introduces C#

The Microsoft solution to this problem is a language called C# (pronounced "C sharp"). C# is a modern, object-oriented language that enables programmers to quickly build a wide range of applications for the new Microsoft .NET platform, which provides tools and services that fully exploit both computing and communications.

Because of its elegant object-oriented design, C# is a great choice for architecting a wide range of components—from high-level business objects to system-level applications. Using simple C# language constructs, these components can be converted into Web services, allowing them to be invoked across the Internet, from any language running on any operating system.

More than anything else, C# is designed to bring rapid development to the C++ programmer without sacrificing the power and control that have been a hallmark of C and C++. Because of this heritage, C# has a high degree of fidelity with C and C++. Developers familiar with these languages can quickly become productive in C#.

Productivity and Safety

The new Web economy—where competitors are just one click away—is forcing businesses to respond to competitive threats faster than ever before. Developers are called upon to shorten cycle times and produce more incremental revisions of a program, rather than a single monumental version.

C# is designed with these considerations in mind. The language is designed to help developers do more with fewer lines of code and fewer opportunities for error.

Embraces emerging Web programming standards

The new model for developing applications means more and more solutions require the use of emerging Web standards like Hypertext Markup Language (HTML), Extensible Markup Language (XML), and Simple Object Access Protocol (SOAP). Existing development tools were developed before the Internet or when the Web as we know it today was in its infancy. As a result, they don't always provide the best fit for working with new Web technologies.

C# programmers can leverage an extensive framework for building applications on the Microsoft .NET platform. C# includes built-in support to turn any component into a Web service that can be invoked over the Internet—from any application running on any platform.

Even better, the Web services framework can make existing Web services look just like native C# objects to the programmer, thus allowing developers to leverage existing Web services with the object-oriented programming skills they already have.

There are more subtle features that make C# a great Internet programming tool. For instance, XML is emerging as the standard way to pass structured data across the Internet. Such data sets are often very small. For improved performance, C# allows the XML data to be mapped directly into a struct data type instead of a class. This is a more efficient way to handle small amounts of data.

Eliminates costly programming errors

Even expert C++ programmers can make the simplest of mistakes—forgetting to initialize a variable, for instance—and often those simple mistakes result in unpredictable problems that can remain undiscovered for long periods of time. Once a program is in production use, it can be very costly to fix even the simplest programming errors.

The modern design of C# eliminates the most common C++ programming errors. For example:

- Garbage collection relieves the programmer of the burden of manual memory management.
- Variables in C# are automatically initialized by the environment.
- Variables are type-safe.

The end result is a language that makes it far easier for developers to write and maintain programs that solve complex business problems.

Reduces ongoing development costs with built-in support for versioning

Updating software components is an error-prone task. Revisions made to the code can unintentionally change the semantics of an existing program. To assist the developer with this problem, C# includes versioning support in the language. For example, method overriding must be explicit; it cannot happen inadvertently as in C++ or Java. This helps prevent coding errors and preserve versioning flexibility. A related feature is the native support for interfaces and interface inheritance. These features enable complex frameworks to be developed and evolved over time.

Put together, these features make the process of developing later versions of a project more robust and thus reduce overall development costs for the successive versions.

Power, Expressiveness, and Flexibility

Better mapping between business process and implementation

With the high level of effort that corporations spend on business planning, it is imperative to have a close connection between the abstract business process and the actual software implementation. But most language tools don't have an easy way to link business logic with code. For instance, developers probably use code comments today to identify which classes make up a particular abstract business object.

The C# language allows for typed, extensible metadata that can be applied to any object. A project architect can define domain-specific attributes and apply them to any language element—classes, interfaces, and so on. The developer then can programmatically examine the attributes on each element. This makes it easy, for example, to write an automated tool that will ensure that each class or interface is correctly identified as part of a particular abstract business object, or simply to create reports based on the domain-specific attributes of an object. The tight coupling between the custom metadata and the program code helps strengthen the connection between the intended program behavior and the actual implementation.

Extensive interoperability

The managed, type-safe environment is appropriate for most enterprise applications. But real-world experience shows that some applications continue to require "native" code, either for performance reasons or to interoperate with existing application programming interfaces (APIs). Such scenarios may force developers to use C++ even when they would prefer to use a more productive development environment.

C# addresses these problems by:

- Including native support for the Component Object Model (COM) and Windows®-based APIs.
- Allowing restricted use of native pointers.

With C#, every object is automatically a COM object. Developers no longer have to explicitly implement IUnknown and other COM interfaces. Instead, those features are built in. Similarly, C# programs can natively use existing COM objects, no matter what language was used to author them.

For those developers who require it, C# includes a special feature that enables a program to call out to any native API. Inside a specially marked code block, developers are allowed to use pointers and traditional C/C++ features such as manually managed memory and pointer arithmetic. This is a huge advantage over other environments. It means that C# programmers can build on their existing C and C++ code base, rather than discard it.

In both cases—COM support and native API access—the goal is to provide the developer with essential power and control without having to leave the C# environment.

Conclusion

C# is a modern, object-oriented language that enables programmers to quickly and easily build solutions for the Microsoft .NET platform. The framework provided allows C# components to become Web services that are available across the Internet, from any application running on any platform.

The language enhances developer productivity while serving to eliminate programming errors that can lead to increased development costs. C# brings rapid Web development to the C and C++ programmer while maintaining the power and flexibility that those developers call for.

Sharp New Language: C# Offers the Power of C++ and Simplicity of Visual Basic

This article by Joshua Trupin, technical editor for MSDN Magazine, was published in the September 2000 issue of MSDN Magazine. C# is a new programming language that answers developers' call for a language that is easy to write, read, and maintain like Visual Basic but that still provides the power and flexibility of C++. Microsoft has built C# with type safety, garbage collection, simplified type declarations, versioning and scalability support, and many other features that make developing solutions faster and easier, particularly for COM+ and Web Services. C# was announced in June 2000 and will be part of the upcoming Visual Studio.NET suite.

You may have read recent press accounts of a new programming language that Microsoft has been developing. Well, the language is here. C#, pronounced "C sharp," is a new programming language that makes it easier for C and C++ programmers to generate COM+-ready programs. In addition, C# lass. C'mon already—you're a smart language. Visual C++® even has IntelliSense®. Clean up after me. If you like C and C++, but sometimes think like I do, C# is for you.

The main design goal of C# was simplicity rather than pure power. You do give up a little processing power, but you get cool stuff like type safety and automatic garbage collection in return. C# can make your code more stable and productive overall, meaning that you can more than make up that lost power in the long run. C# offers several key benefits for programmers:

- Simplicity
- Consistency
- Modernity
- Object-orientation
- Type-safety
- Scalability
- Version support
- Compatibility
- Flexibility

Let's look at each of the ways that C# stands to improve your coding life.

Simplicity

What's one of the most annoying things about working in C++? It's gotta be remembering when to use the -> pointer indicator, when to use the :: for a class member, and when to use the dot. And the compiler knows when you get it wrong, doesn't it? It even tells you that you got it wrong! If there's a reason for that beyond out-and-outtaunting, I fail to see it.

C# recognizes this irksome little fixture of the C++ programming life and simplifies it. In C#, *everything* is represented by a dot. Whether you're looking at members, classes, name-spaces, references, or what have you, you don't need to track which operator to use.

Okay, so what's the second most annoying thing about working in C and C++? It's figuring out exactly what type of data type to use. In C#, a Unicode character is no longer a wchar_t, it's a char. A 64-bit integer is a long, not an __int64. And a char is a char is a char. There's no more char, unsigned char, signed char, and wchar_t to track. I'll talk more about data types later in this article.

The third most annoying problem that you run across in C and C++ is integers being used as Booleans, causing assignment errors when you confuse = and ==. C# separates these two types, providing a separate bool type that solves this problem. A bool can be true or false, and can't be converted into other types. Similarly, an integer or object reference can't be tested to be true or false—it must be compared to zero (or to null in the case of the reference). If you wrote code like this in C++:

```
int i;
if (i) . . .
```

You need to convert that into something like this for C#:

```
int i;
if (i != 0) . . .
```

Another programmer-friendly feature is the improvement over C++ in the way switch statements work. In C++, you could write a switch statement that fell through from case to case. For example, this code

```
switch (i)
{
  case 1:
    FunctionA();

  case 2:
    FunctionB();
    Break;
}
```

would call both FunctionA and FunctionB if i was equal to 1. C# works like Visual Basic, putting an implied break before each case statement. If you really do want the case statement to fall through, you can rewrite the switch block like this in C#:

```
switch (i)      .
{
  case 1:
    FunctionA();
    goto case 2;

  case 2:
    FunctionB();
    Break;
}
```

Consistency

C# unifies the type system by letting you view every type in the language as an object. Whether you're using a class, a struct, an array, or a primitive, you'll be able to treat it as an object. Objects are combined into namespaces, which allow you to access everything programmatically. This means that instead of putting includes in your file like this

```
#include <stdlib.h>
#include <stdio.h>
#include <string.h>
```

you include a particular namespace in your program to gain access to the classes and objects contained within it:

```
using System;
```

In COM+, all classes exist within a single hierarchical namespace. In C#, the using statement lets you avoid having to specify the fully qualified name when you use a class. For example, the System namespace contains sev-eralclasses, including Console. Console has a WriteLine method that, as you might expect, writes a line to the system console. If you want to write the output part of a Hello World program in C#, you can say:

```
System.Console.WriteLine("Hello World!");
```

This same code can be written as:

```
Using System;
Console.WriteLine("Hello World!");
```

That's almost everything you need for the C# Hello World program. A complete C# program needs a class definition and a Main function. A complete, console-based Hello World program in C# looks like this:

```
using System;

class HelloWorld
{
  public static int Main(String[] args)
  {
    Console.WriteLine("Hello, World!");
    return 0;
  }
}
```

The first line makes System—the COM+ base class namespace—available to the program. The program class itself is named HelloWorld (code is arranged into classes, not by files). The Main method (which takes arguments) is defined within HelloWorld. The COM+ Console class writes the friendly message, and the program is finished.

Of course, you could get fancy. What if you want to reuse the HelloWorld program? Easy—put it into its own namespace! Just wrap it in a namespace and declare the classes as public if you want them accessible outside the particular namespace. (Note here that I've changed the name Main to the more suitable name SayHi.)

```
using System;

namespace MSDNMag
{
  public class HelloWorld
  {
    public static int SayHi()
    {
      Console.WriteLine("Hello, World!");
      return 0;
    }
  }
}
```

You can then compile this into a DLL, and include the DLL with any other programs you're building. The calling program could look like this:

```
using System;
using MSDNMag;

class CallingMSDNMag
{
  public static void Main(string[] args)
  {
    elloWorld.SayHi();
    return 0;
  }
}
```

One final point about classes. If you have classes with the same name in more than one namespace, C# lets you define aliases for any of them so you don't have to fully qualify them. Here's an example. Suppose you have created a class NS1.NS2. ClassA that looks like this:

```
namespace NS1.NS2
{
  class ClassA {}
}
```

You can then create a second namespace, NS3, that derives the class N3.ClassB from NS1.NS2.ClassA like this:

```
namespace NS3
{
  class ClassB: NS1.NS2.ClassA {}
}
```

If this construct is too long for you, or if you're going to repeat it several times, you can use the alias A for the class NS1.NS2.ClassA with the using statement like so:

```
namespace NS3
{
  using A = NS1.NS2.ClassA;
  class ClassB: A {}
}
```

This effect can be accomplished at any level of an object hierarchy. For instance, you could also create an alias for NS1.NS2
like this:

```
namespace NS3
{
  using C = NS1.NS2;
  class ClassB: C.A {}
}
```

Modernity

Like coding languages, the needs of programmers evolve over time. What was once revolutionary is now sort of, well, dated. Like that old Toyota Corolla on the neighbor's lawn, C and C++ provide reliable transportation, but lack some of the features that people look for when they kick the tires. This is one of the reasons many developers have tinkered with the Java language over the past few years.

C# goes back to the drawing board and emerges with several features that I longed for in C++. Garbage collection is one example—everything gets cleaned up when it's no longer referenced. However, garbage collection can have a price. It makes problems caused by certain risky behavior (using unsafe casts and stray pointers, for example) far harder to diagnose and potentially more devastating to a program. To compensate for this, C# implements type safety to ensure application stability. Of course, type safety also makes your code more readable, so others on your team can see what you've been up to—you take the bad with the good, I guess. I'll go into this later in this article.

C# has a richer intrinsic model for error handling than C++. Have you ever really gotten deep into a coworker's code? It's amazing—there are dozens of unchecked HRESULTs all over the place, and when a call fails, the program always ends up displaying an "Error: There was an error" message. C# improves on this situation by providing integral support for throw, try…catch, and try…finally as language elements. True, you could do this as a macro in C++, but now it's available right out of the box.

Part of a modern language is the ability to actually use it for something. It seems simple enough, but many languages completely ignore the needs for financial and time-based data types. They're too old economy or something. Borrowing from languages like SQL, C# implements built-in support for data types like decimal and string, and lets you implement new primitive types that are as efficient as the existing ones. I'll discuss some of the new support for data types and arrays later in the article.

You'll also be glad to see that C# takes a more modern approach to debugging. The traditional way to write a debuggable program in C++ was to sprinkle it with #ifdefs and indicate that large sections of code would only be executed during the debugging process. You would end up with two implementations—a debug build and a retail build, with some of the calls in the retail build going to functions that do nothing. C# offers the conditional keyword to control program flow based on defined tokens.

Remember the MSDNMag namespace? A single conditional statement can make the SayHi member a debug-only function.

```
using System;

namespace MSDNMag
{
  public class HelloWorld
  {
    [conditional("DEBUG")]
    public static void SayHi()
    {
      Console.WriteLine("Hello, World!");
      return;
    }
    ...
  }
}
```

Conditional functions must have void return types (as I've set in this sample). The client program would then have to look like this to get a Hello World message:

```
using System
using MSDNMag

#define DEBUG

class CallingMSDNMag
{
  public static void Main(string[] args)
  {
    HelloWorld.SayHi();
    return 0;
  }
}
```

The code is nice and uncluttered without all those #ifdefs hanging around, waiting to be ignored.

Finally, C# is designed to be easy to parse, so vendors can create tools that allow source browsing and two-way code generation.

Object Oriented

Yeah, yeah. C++ is object oriented. Right. I've personally known people who have worked on multiple inheritance for a week, then retired out of frustration to North Carolina to clean hog lagoons. That's why C# ditches multiple inheritance in favor of native support for the COM+ virtual object system. Encapsulation, polymorphism, and inheritance are preserved without all the pain.

C# ditches the entire concept of global functions, variables, and constants. Instead, you can createstaticclassmembers, making C# code easier to read and less prone to naming conflicts.

And speaking of naming conflicts, have you ever forgotten that you created a class member and redefined it later on in your code? By default, C# methods are nonvirtual, requiring an explicit virtual modifier. It's far harder to accidentally override a method, it's easier to provide correct versioning, and the vtable doesn't grow as quickly. Class members in C# can be defined as private, protected, public, or internal. You retain full control over their encapsulation.

Methods and operators can be overloaded in C#, using a syntax that's a lot easier than the one used by C++. However, you can't overload global operator functions—the overloading is strictly local in scope. The overloading of method F below is an example of what this looks like:

```
interface ITest
{
   void F();            // F()
   void F(int x);       // F(int)
   void F(ref int x);   // F(ref int)
   void F(out int x);   // F(out int)
   void F(int x, int y); // F(int, int)
   int F(string s);     // F(string)
   int F(int x);        // F(int)
}
```

The COM+ component model is supported through the implementation of delegates—the object-oriented equivalent of function pointers in C++.

Interfaces support multiple inheritance. Classes can privately implement internal interfaces through explicit member implementations, without the consumer ever knowing about it.

Type Safety

Although some power users would disagree with me, type safety promotes robust programs. Several features that promote proper code execution (and more robust programs) in Visual Basic have been included in C#. For example, all dynamically allocated objects and arrays are initialized to zero. Although C# doesn't automatically initialize local variables, the compiler will warn you if you use one before you initialize it. When you access an array, it is automatically range checked. Unlike C and C++, you can't overwrite unallocated memory.

In C# you can't create an invalid reference. All casts are required to be safe, and you can't cast between integer and reference types. Garbage collection in C# ensures that you don't leave references dangling around your code. Hand-in-hand with this feature is overflow checking. Arithmetic operations and conversions are not allowed if they overflow the target variable or object. Of course, there are some valid reasons to want a variable to overflow. If you do, you can explicitly disable the checking.

As I've mentioned, the data types supported in C# are somewhat different from what you might be used to in C++. For instance, the char type is 16 bits. Certain useful types, like decimal and string, are built in. Perhaps the biggest difference between C++ and C#, however, is the way C# handles arrays.

C# arrays are managed types, meaning that they hold references, not values, and they're garbage collected. You can declare arrays in several ways, including as multidimensional (rectangular) arrays and as arrays of arrays (jagged). Note in the following examples that the square brackets come after the type, not after the identifier as in some languages.

```
int[ ] intArray;              // A simple array
int[ , , ] intArray;          // A multidimensional array of rank 3 (3
                              // dimensions)
int[ ][ ] intArray            // A jagged array of arrays
int[ ][ , , ][ , ] intArray;  // A single-dimensional array of three-
                              // dimensional arrays of two-dimensional
                              // arrays
```

Arrays are actually objects; when you first declare them they don't have a size. For this reason, you must create them after you declare them. Suppose you want an array of size 5. This code will do the trick:

```
int[] intArray = new int[5];
```

If you do this twice, it automatically reallocates the array. Therefore

```
int[] intArray;
intArray = new int[5];
intArray = new int[10];
```

results in an array called intArray, which has 10 members. Instantiating a rectangular array is similarly easy:

```
int[] intArray = new int[3,4];
```

However, instantiating a jagged array needs a bit more work. You might expect to say new int[3][4], but you really need to say:

```
int[][] intArray = new int[3][];
For (int a = 0; a < intArray.Length; a++) {
  intArray[a] = new intArray[4];
}
```

You can initialize a statement in the same line you create and instantiate it by using curly brackets:

```
int[] intArray = new int[5] {1, 2, 3, 4, 5};
```

You can do the same thing with a string-based array:

```
string[] strArray = new string[3] {"MSJ", "MIND","MSDNMag"};
```

If you mix brackets, you can initialize a multidimensional array:

```
int[,] intArray = new int[3, 2] { {1, 2}, {3, 4}, {5, 6} };
```

You can also initialize a jagged array:

```
int[][] intArray = new int[][] { new int[] {2,3,4}, new int[] {5,6,7} };
```

If you leave out the new operator, you can even initialize an array with implicit dimensions:

```
int[] intArray = {1, 2, 3, 4, 5};
```

Arrays are considered objects in C#, and as such they are handled like objects, not like an addressable stream of bytes. Specifically, arrays are automatically garbage collected, so you don't need to destroy them when you're finished using them. Arrays are based on the C# class System.Array, so you can treat them conceptually like a collection object, using their Length property and looping through each item in the array. If you define intArray as shown earlier, the call

```
intArray.Length
```

would return 5. The System.Array class also provides ways to copy, sort, and search arrays.

C# provides a foreach operator, which operates like its counterpart in Visual Basic, letting you loop through an array. Consider this snippet:

```
int[] intArray = {2, 4, 6, 8, 10, -2, -3, -4, 8};
foreach (int i in intArray)
{
   System.Console.WriteLine(i);
}
```

This code will print each number in intArray on its own line of the system console. The System.Array class also provides a GetLength member function, so the preceding code could also be written like this (remember, arrays are zero-based in C#):

```
for (int i = 0; i < intArray.GetLength(); i++)
{
   System.Console.WriteLine(i);
}
```

Scalability

C and C++ require all sorts of often-incompatible header files before you can compile all but the simplest code. C# gets rid of these frequently aggravating headers by combining the declaration and definition of types. It also directly imports and emits COM+ metadata, making incrementalcompiles much easier.

When a project gets large enough, you might want to split up your code into smaller source files. C# doesn't have any restrictions about where your source files live or what they're named. When you compile a C# project, you can think of it as concatenating all the source files, then compiling them into one big file. You don't have to track which headers go where, or which routines belong in which source file. This also means that you can move, rename, split, or merge source files without breaking your compile.

Version Support

DLL Hell is a constant problem for users and programmers alike. MSDN® Online has even dedicated a service specifically for users who need to track the different versions of system DLLs. There's nothing a programming language can do to keep a library author from messing around with a published API. However, C# was designed to make versioning far easier by retaining binary compatibility with existing derived classes. When you introduce a new member in a base class as one that exists in a derived class, it doesn't cause an error. However, the designer of the class must indicate whether the method is meant as an override or as a new method that just hides the similar inherited method.

As I've already mentioned, C# works with a namespace model. Classes and interfaces in class libraries must be defined in hierarchical namespaces instead of in a flat model. Applications can explicitly import a single member of a namespace, so there won't be any collisions when multiple namespaces contain similarly named members. When you declare a namespace, subsequent declarations are considered to be part of the same declaration space. Therefore, if your code looks like this

```
namespace MSDNMag.Article
{
  class Author
  {
    ...
  }
}
```

(continued)

(continued)

```
namespace MSDNMag.Article
{
  class Topic
  {
    ...
  }
}
```

you could express the same code like so:

```
namespace MSDNMag.Article
{
  class Author
  {
    ...
  }

  class Topic
  {
    ...
  }
}
```

Compatibility

Four types of APIs are common on the Windows platform and C# supports all of them. The old-style C APIs have integrated support in C#. Applications can use the N/Direct features of COM+ to call C-style APIs. C# provides transparent access to standard COM and OLE Automation APIs and supports all data types through the COM+ runtime. Most importantly, C# supports the COM+ Common Language Subset specification. If you've exported any entities that aren't accessible from another language, the compiler can optionally flag the code. For instance, a class can't have two members runJob and runjob because a case-insensitive language would choke on the definitions.

When you call a DLL export, you need to declare the method, attach a sysimport attribute, and specify any custom marshaling and return value information that overrides the COM+ defaults. The following shows how to write a Hello World program that displays its message of cheer in a standard Windows message box.

```
class HelloWorld
{
  [sysimport(dll = "user32.dll")]
  public static extern int MessageBoxA(int h, string m,
                                       string c, int type);

  public static int Main()
  {
    return MessageBoxA(0, "Hello World!", "Caption", 0);
  }
}
```

Each COM+ type maps to a default native data type, which COM+ uses to marshal values across a native API call. The C# string value maps to the LPSTR type by default, but it can be overridden with marshaling statements like so:

```
using System;
using System.Interop;

class HelloWorld
{
  [dllimport("user32.dll")]
  public static extern int MessageBoxW(
    int h,
    [marshal(UnmanagedType.LPWStr)] string m,
    [marshal(UnmanagedType.LPWStr)] string c,
    int type);

  public static int Main()
  {
    return MessageBoxW(0, "Hello World!", "Caption", 0);
  }
}
```

In addition to working with DLL exports, you can work with classic COM objects in several ways: create them with CoCreateInstance, query them for interfaces, and call methods on them.

If you want to import a COM class definition for use within your program, you must take two steps. First, you must create a class and use the comimport attribute to mark it as related to a specific GUID. The class you create can't have any base classes or interface lists, nor can it have any members.

```
// declare FilgraphManager as a COM classic coclass
[comimport, guid("E436EBB3-524F-11CE-9F53-0020AF0BA770")]
class FilgraphManager
{
}
```

After the class is declared in your program, you can create a new instance of it with the new keyword (which is equivalent to the CoCreateInstance function).

```
class MainClass
{
  public static void Main()
  {
    FilgraphManager f = new FilgraphManager();
  }
}
```

You can query interfaces indirectly in C# by attempting to cast an object to a new interface. If the cast fails, it will throw a System.InvalidCastException. If it works, you'll have an object that represents that interface.

```
FilgraphManager graphManager = new FilgraphManager();
IMediaControl mc = (IMediaControl) graphManager;
mc.Run(); // If the cast succeeds, this line will work.
```

Flexibility

It's true that C# and COM+ create a managed, type-safe environment. However, it's also true that some real-world applications need to get to the native code level—either for performance considerations or to use old-style, unmodernized APIs from other programs. I've discussed ways to use APIs and COM components from your C# program. C# lets you declare unsafe classes and methods that contain pointers, structs, and static arrays. These methods won't be type-safe, but they will execute within the managed space so you don't have to marshal boundaries between safe and unsafe code.

These unsafe features are integrated with the COM+ EE and code access security in COM+. This means that a developer can pin an object so that the garbage collector will pass over them when it's doing its work. (Sort of like a mezuzah for your code.) Unsafe code won't be executed outside a fully trusted environment. Programmers can even turn off garbage collection while an unsafe method is executing.

Availability

C# was announced in June and will be part of the upcoming Visual Studio.NET suite. A compiler is expected to be available later this year, in advance of the release of the next generation of Visual Studio®.

Programming in C#: Technobabble

In this interview transcript, Anders Hejlsberg, Distinguished Engineer at Microsoft Corporation, discusses C# and how it affects the development process. The interview was published in fall 2000 on the .NET Show on MSDN Online. Topics discussed include the origins and goals of C#, how the new language includes the concept of component-oriented programming and also makes it simpler to write applications, the extent to which ideas were borrowed from other languages, differences in how code is written in C#, how C# helps preserve developers' intellectual property rights, interoperability among different languages, the effort to have C# standardized by a European standards body called ECMA, how developers should conceptually work their applications in order to better use C#, and the parallel evolution of C#, XML, and SOAP.

Robert Hess: Welcome back. Now, like any platform you develop applications for, one of the primary things you need in order to get those applications to actually run, is a language. Now, .NET has a special language that we've developed for it called C#. With me here today is Anders Hejlsberg, he's a distinguished engineer at Microsoft, and he played a pivotal role in the C# language, as well as in the .NET platform. You've all seen him before on the show, and so I brought him back to come talk with us about C#, what it is, and what programmers can take advantage of with it, and how it really affects the development of applications.

So, what exactly have you done with C#, and when did you get started working with it?

Anders Hejlsberg: Well, we've been working on C# for the last, probably, two and a half years. It's been a design group of four people, and it's been my major focus for those two and a half years. There are many things we wanted to do with a new programming language, you know. I think primarily, probably, is simplify life for programmers, making programmers more productive is ultimately what it comes down to. Now, that gain in productivity sort of takes many shapes, but you could say that we've targeted, with C#, in a sense, the power and expressiveness of C++, but with the ease of use and productivity of RAD (Rapid Application Development) languages. Some of the things we've done, for example, come into the categories of giving programmers access to a better tool for writing components. If you look at how we write applications, or actually, if you look at how we used to write applications, if you go back, say five or ten years, it used to be that applications were built as sort of these big monolithical things and about the only interaction it had with the operating system other than, you know, doing file i/o and whatever it was that the operating system would launch it, and then the user would interact with the application, and shut it down again.

If you look at how we build applications today, for the internet, it's actually a very different world. Apps are not monolithical things, rather they are sort of composed of a bunch of smaller components that sit in various hosting environments. You might have components such as stored procedures and SQL Server, you might have controls hosted in a browser, you might have code sitting in an ASP page. Business objects living on a middle tier, and you called sort of that whole congregation of components your application. Now in order to make that...

Robert Hess: And when you make it, each one of those components is more complex than an application used to be five or ten years ago.

Anders Hejlsberg: Oh, absolutely, absolutely. And so, to make them less complex to build, unlike big monolithical applications, you don't want to start from scratch every time you have to build one of these components. Rather you want to sort of be able to inherit from something that already exists in the particular hosting environment; you want to inherit from a base control. If you're writing a control in a browser, you want to inherit from some core business object class if you're writing a business object on the middle tier, and you want to expose things from these components like properties and methods and events, and you want to say something about how they integrate with the hosting environment through attributes that you attach to the component. And you want to be able to write documentation for the components, along side with the components.

Robert Hess: All this is just standard object oriented programming that's been around for quite some time with Smalltalk, and...

Anders Hejlsberg: Well, absolutely, and it's not that you can't do these things today. But if you look at the programming languages that are in widespread use today, they don't actually really support component-oriented concepts. If you look at, say, C++, when, well, if first you accept that when we talk about components it is very common today to think of them as having properties and methods and events. But if you look at C++, there is really only notion of methods. There are no properties. There are no events. Now, you can emulate them by having naming patterns that says, you know, for a property, instead of having a color property you have a getColor and a setColor method. And instead of having events as a first class member in a class, you have interfaces that someone wanting to receive the event has to implement, and so there's a bunch of housekeeping that you have to go through, in order to do that.

Robert Hess: Well, part of it is just because C++ is based on C, and it's just like a preprocessor thing, so since C didn't support that inherently, C++ couldn't...

Anders Hejlsberg: Yeah, I actually sort of think that what you're seeing is an evolution from C to C++ to C#. From C to C++, the concept of object oriented programming was added. If you go from C++ to C#, I would say that the concept of component oriented programming has been added, and there's really an analogy. Just like you could do object oriented programming in C, instead of C++, so can you do component oriented programming in C++ instead of C#. It's just harder. It's a lot harder in C to do object oriented programming, you have to manually lay out your V tables and do all sorts of housekeeping, and the same is true in C++. You can write components, but you have to manually, sort of, have naming patterns for your properties; you have to manually implement event syncs; you have to have external IDL files where you describe your hosting attributes; you have to have external documentation files, and so forth. And we really are just sort of taking that next logical step that reflects how people write applications, and folding it into the language. So you get one stop programming, so to speak.

Robert Hess: So then, what were some of the initial objectives, just for a mental thinking standpoint, when you first started this project, of the problems you wanted to solve and directions you wanted to take this new language?

Anders Hejlsberg: Well, I think, as you said, the component orientation was one thing. I think another key factor is simplification. Just make it simpler to write applications, don't make programmers do the housekeeping that the machine could do for you. Now, a lot of that simplification lies in the .NET runtime itself, but a lot of it lies in the language as well. And basically, in the end, what we do is we give you more time to focus on the algorithms, and we let the system do the housekeeping. I think, a couple of other things that were very key, was sort of the realization that we can't just tell people to throw away all of their existing code. We have to find a way to leverage, not just your skills, but also the code that you've written before, that exists already. So, in terms of leveraging your skills we've tried to stay very close and very true to the underlying syntax of C++, in C#. So any C++ programmer will immediately feel familiar and at home with C#.

Robert Hess: Now was that one of the original thoughts, you were going to take and do something that was one step above C, or did you originally think, let's just throw out everything, let's just start with a brand new language?

Anders Hejlsberg: Well, I think we did start with a blank slate, but we knew that we wanted C and C++ programmers to feel familiar with this language. That, of course, meant that, sort of, statement structure, we weren't going to go change that from being curly braces to being something else. You know, so there was sort of a foundation laid there already. But there were some other key tenets, like allowing you to write robust software, and that means things like garbage collection, exception handling, type safety, that fundamentally alter how you design the language, and are very hard to come in and sprinkle on later. I mean, in C++ one of the strengths of the C++ language, but also sometimes one of the hard parts about it is the fact that, there is no type safety.

Now, if you know what you're doing, that gives you tremendous power, but if you don't, you know, you can get in trouble. It is very easy in C++ to have a dangling pointer. It's very easy to overwrite over the end of an array, or to have an uninitialized variable, and so forth. And we wanted to solve some of those problems. And I think that you can't just start with C++ and sprinkle it on. You really have to sort of take a step back, and then continue, but create your design in the spirit of C++, which is sort of what we've done.

Robert Hess: What about other languages, did you look at what other languages were doing, whether it's Pascal, or Modular 2, or FORTH, and borrow things from those?

Anders Hejlsberg: Absolutely. Oh, we looked at, I mean, well, I come myself from a strong Pascal background, so, naturally, you know, looking at Pascal, Modula, Oberon, and looking at Smalltalk, looked at Java, looked at C++, looked at a whole range of languages that exist and are in use today, more or less widespread.

Robert Hess: What are some of the features in those languages that you felt they were doing something better than C and C++ where that you needed to bring into this new language?

Anders Hejlsberg: Well, I think, one of the things that I, for example, always have liked about Smalltalk, is the notion that, in that language, everything is an object. Now, this gives you tremendous simplification, because it doesn't matter what piece of data you're holding, you can carry it from point A to point B as an object. Anything can sort of operate on it generically. You can put it in a container, just typed as object. Now, in the actual implementation in Smalltalk there are some pretty heavy performance overhead associated with how they do it. For example, in Smalltalk, when you operate on floating point numbers, for every new number you produce, you know, when you add 1.0 and 2.0 together, you allocate a new object that contains the value 3.0. And that's, of course, a very expensive way of doing it. Now, we've done some innovative work in C# that allows you to get the same benefits, but without the overhead. As long as you treat your floats as floats, you know, if you say, or double, you used the type double, there is no cost. But you can treat them as objects, and at that point they get heap allocated, but only if you do so. So there are some nice unification there that gives you a lot of the benefits without the performance overhead.

Robert Hess: What about some of the structures of the end result of what happens out of C#? So you've got this text file C# program and you compile it, what about some of the issues of the compiler itself, how are some of the designs built into that to be more effective in use with what some of the other languages might have done, and even the binary executable that comes out at the bottom end?

Anders Hejlsberg: Well, we've done some things with respect to just how you write your code. If you're a C++ programmer, you're of course familiar with how you have, in C++, a separation of declaration and implementation. So you write all your declarations in H files that you then pound include in other modules, and then you write your actually implementation in CPP files. In C# you write both in the same place. So you write your declaration and then you immediately write your code in there as well.

Robert Hess: Then what if you need to take and use some values declared in your main file in some other file?

Anders Hejlsberg: So what happens then, when you compile, that instead of just producing X86 machine code that has nothing but the executable code in it, we actually produce code or reproduce an output file that has both the code, and the metadata, the symbol tables, or the associated symbolic information. In a sense the code becomes self describing. So when you want to use one piece of code from another piece of code, you simply reference that other code, and the code is self describing enough that you know what classes are in there, what members the classes have, what are the methods you can call, what are the properties, what are the type names, etc., etc.

Robert Hess: So would that be like you're pointing at the .OBJ file or the .EXE file, or...?

Anders Hejlsberg: Well, the format we use in .NET is a PE format, so you could point at another EXE or at another DLL. We call those assemblies now, and we basically use that word sort of broadly to describe these super DLLs, if you will, that contain not just code, but also information that talks about what is in the code, and also, indeed, talks about what other assemblies this code references.

Robert Hess: And by code you mean binary code or executable code.

Anders Hejlsberg: Well, actually, we don't produce directly executable X86 machine code, rather we produce MSIL, which is the intermediate language that .NET defines and that it provides JIT (Just In Time) compilers for.

Robert Hess: Ok, so, you've got an executable, per se, that is this intermediate language as well as the metadata associated to it, and if I want to use that in one of my applications, I just point to it and say, hey, I want to borrow these classes, borrow these objects, and use it in my own thing like that. This reminds me of a problem I've heard a couple of people mention, is that there is a concern that if they got an intermediate language, that the potential exists that someone else can take and grab that file and decompile it, and get back to the original source code, and therefore, null all the intellectual property rights associated with the developer. What are some of the issues there?

Anders Hejlsberg: Well, first of all, you can actually do that with DLLs today. It's just probably a bit harder, but you could take a DLL containing X86 machine code, and decompile it into assembler, at least. You can do the same...

Robert Hess: I used to do that on my Apple II all the time.

Anders Hejlsberg: Exactly, I'm guilty of it. But you could to the same with .NET DLLs, and decompile them into MSIL. They're not decompileable directly into C#, although you could probably also finagle that problem, it's much harder. Now, the thing that's different is, there's a lot more symbolic information associated with the code produced by C#, along with MSIL, I'm sorry, a .NET assembly.

For example, you can learn from the code what classes are in here, what are their members, and so forth. It's a tough problem to solve, because there are so many advantages to having the code be self describing, but the fact that the code carries around a description of itself, also makes it somewhat easier to understand what the code does with a decompilation tool. Now if we're looking at this problem, basically what we're looking to do is build what's known as an obfuscator, you know, that will go in and mangle your code around so it becomes next to illegible, yet still preserves the same public interface.

Robert Hess: Yeah, because the problem you've got is that you want that code to be understandable by compilers, and so forth, like that, but you don't want them to be understandable at that same level by individuals, when you take and write these compiler programs.

Anders Hejlsberg: Exactly, exactly. Now, I do want to point out that, for a small application, it might actually be possible for you to decompile it and, given enough time and resources, you could even understand what it does. For a real world application, this is quite an undertaking, and in reality you're probably better off running the app, understanding what it does, and then writing a copy of it, you know. You'd get there sooner.

Robert Hess: Probably write a better program anyway, because you're a better programmer, right? What are some of the issues about C# that our audience might need to understand in order to figure out whether they want to start implementing their next project in C# or not?

Anders Hejlsberg: Well, I think first of all, you need to think about where you're coming from. If you have an existing body of code, and let's say that it's written in C++ already, probably your shortest path to moving that code to the .NET Framework is to use Managed C++, the C++ compiler that we're shipping with .NET. However, if you're looking at writing new code, be that either, you know, sort of new modules, larger modules that go into an application, or a whole know application, and you are skilled in C++, then, I would recommend that you look at C#.

Robert Hess: So, we're not necessarily saying that everybody needs to rewrite their applications in C#. We're saying that people need to understand the type of project they're currently working on, whether it is an existing project, legacy code, and sometimes, write some of those components in C#, but that you can use C# and C++ interchangeable?

Anders Hejlsberg: Oh, well, absolutely. First of all, if you just have existing code that is written, say, using really any language that is supported by, you know, the Windows platform today, compiled either into COM component or into DLLs, we give you great interoperability with that code. Now, if you're writing code specifically for the .NET Framework, new code for the .NET Framework, you can indeed write it in any of the languages that are supported by the .NET Framework.

We're going to be shipping four languages with Visual Studio.NET: C#, C++, Visual Basic, and JScript. But in cooperation with the industry and academia, I think, at latest count, this may not be a precise count, but I think the total is at about 17 different languages now targeting that platform, ranging all the way from, you know, APL to Cobol.

Robert Hess: What about something like Fortran?

Anders Hejlsberg: I believe there is work in progress for, I don't know precisely who's building that Fortran compiler. But the key thing here is, and we've actually, we've demonstrated that many times, but you could write a base class in C#, inherit from it in C++, and use a VB program to create instances of it. It's that seamless to do that interoperability between the different languages. And that's something that I think really sets apart the .NET Framework from other, you know, other competitive products in the industry.

Robert Hess: And that it takes and allows multiple language to interoperate on level footing.

Anders Hejlsberg: Exactly, yes. But at a very high level. I mean, you could argue that today languages can interoperate. It's just at a very low level with, you know, DLL entry points, structs with pointers in them, or whatever, and we're talking about a much higher semantic level at the object oriented level, if you will, with classes and interfaces and so forth.

Robert Hess: Is C# considered a proprietary language for Microsoft?

Anders Hejlsberg: Actually, no. We, in cooperation with industry partners and in particular with HP and Intel, made a proposal to a European standards organization called ECMA, earlier this year, to standardize C# and something called the CLI which stands for the Common Language Infrastructure.

Robert Hess: And that's similar kind of to the C Runtime and the VB Runtime?

Anders Hejlsberg: Well, actually it is a large subset of the .NET Framework. It is, in a sense, all of those parts of .NET that could be moved to other platforms. Meaning that, for example, it does not include, you know, any Windows specific UI library, for example, because that would not be of much interest to other platforms.

Robert Hess: Things like memory management, and...

Anders Hejlsberg: Well, absolutely, memory management, you know, a large portion of the class library is included in the CLI. We made this proposal to ECMA in September, it was adopted at an ECMA meeting, and work is now underway to formulate these two standards. One for C# and one for a Common Language Infrastructure.

Robert Hess: What does it mean, then, for C# to be a standard through ECMA then?

Anders Hejlsberg: Well, it means that other industry partners can and most likely will go implement this language on different platforms.

Robert Hess: So if I was someone like Boeing or something like that, and I had some, you know, old PDP 11/70, and I wanted to get C# running on it, I could take it upon myself to use the ECMA standards and create my own compiler for my old legacy computers if somebody else wasn't already going to be doing that sort of thing.

Anders Hejlsberg: Absolutely. Now, C#, now the two standards are actually submitted hand in hand, and C# itself currently doesn't specify a runtime library, rather it relies on the .NET Framework, or, when we're talking about the standards submission, it relies on the Common Language Infrastructure to provide the runtime infrastructure and the class libraries for the language. We're currently working with the standardization organization and our industry partners to determine precisely what the lowest bar is of requirement this is going to be. Obviously the CLI will be divided into various levels, indeed the submission that we gave to ECMA is divided into various levels starting at a very low kernel level, but really you just have some of the core data types, some very simple things like arrays, and all of those sort of the atoms are there, but, you know, the molecules are not necessarily there, they're built in higher levels of the stack, and so for embedded devices, you could actually end up with a very lightweight environment that you could move to different platforms.

Robert Hess: So a version of C# that I could run on my wristwatch or something like that.

Anders Hejlsberg: Well in theory, yes, or your refrigerator, or where ever you...

Robert Hess: And that, to a certain extent, is the whole goal of the .NET Framework, is allowing this programming infrastructure to exist on different types of devices so that one device can talk to another device, and borrowing the services and support across them, either connected via network or bluetooth or something like that.

Anders Hejlsberg: Well, yes, that's part of it. I think, now, it's important to keep in mind though that when you talk about distributed applications or devices talking to each other that the infrastructure that we put in place in the .NET Framework and indeed also in CLI, actually does not depend on .NET being present on both ends of the wire. Rather, the architecture that we recommend and indeed leads you towards when you use our class libraries to build your applications is entirely based on industry standards like XML and SOAP, and you can indeed implement it on a Linux box, say, which Java and an Apache web server, and build that other side of the equation using other tools, if you like.

Robert Hess: So in my C# application, if I was writing it to connect to an external service, I could treat the just standard C# calls and so forth, and then an external service running on a different machine could be, you know, Amazon.com, or some other system like that that's not running Windows, not running C#...

Anders Hejlsberg: That is precisely the whole vision of web services...

Robert Hess: And all that would do is just implement SOAP.

Anders Hejlsberg: Yes. Well, basically what we would do is use the existing internet infrastructure, meaning, you know, the carrying protocol is http, the payload is SOAP formatted XML, and indeed there could be anything on the other side of the wire. Now, we will actually, we have the ability to make this XML and the SOAP calls look like objects with methods when you access them from C#, but, we give you all the infrastructure to turn method calls into XML SOAP bodies that go across the wire and come back and get unpackaged again through all of the serialization infrastructure that we have in the .NET Framework.

Robert Hess: Now, you were saying you'd been working in C# for a couple of years now, and, you know, XML had about the same life cycle. So that means that neither one of them kind of knew about the other when they got started.

Anders Hejlsberg: Well, XML's probably been around a little longer than that. SOAP is fairly new and has evolved in parallel with C# and in parallel with the .NET Framework, and we are actively heavily involved in these standardization bodies through the W3C, and we are tracking that, and you know, will continuously adhere to the latest standards.

Robert Hess: So was this level of interconnectivity between SOAP and XML, was that originally one of the aspects of C#, or is that something that kind of evolved as the language evolved?

Anders Hejlsberg: Well, I think, there's actually sort of a separation here. Most of the infrastructure that is required to do XML and SOAP is provided by the .NET Framework, not by the C# language. Now, the C# language builds on top of the .NET Framework and gives you great access to these things, for example, through this thing that we have in C# called attributes, you can directly, in your code, express, you know, what is the mapping from this class instance to an XML formatted body that goes across the Internet. So I can, for example, say, for this field, I would like this field to become this XML element with this name, I would like this class name to become this tag name in XML, and so forth. And we allow you to do that directly integrated in your source code through attributes, so that's one of the things that makes it a lot easier to use XML with C#.

Robert Hess: So they just fit really well together?

Anders Hejlsberg: They do indeed, yes.

Robert Hess: When thinking about the design of an application, is there a different way I want to conceptually work my application up in order to use C# better, or is it just the same sort of mental flow that I'd normally have in a C application?

Anders Hejlsberg: Well, I think one of the key tenets is that you are now programming in a deeply object oriented fashion, and even in a component oriented fashion when you're using C#. So you might tend to think of your application design a little differently.

Now, if you're using C++ you would probably still think of, you know, writing objects and so forth. When you're writing in C#, you may, for example, think about, gees, am I writing a component? Well, is this component going to need to have the ability to go on a toolbox in Visual Studios so I can drag it onto a form or onto a business object or onto a web page, and is it then going to be shown at a property inspector, well gees, then what properties should I have in there, and how do I control what goes in the dropdown list, and should I have a special editor for that? Now, we give you all of that infrastructure, you know, but it makes you think about your design differently than you traditionally would when you just wrote C++ code.

Robert Hess: So, for the most part, you're still writing an application, you just have more capabilities to expose depending on how you embellish your application.

Anders Hejlsberg: You could say that, yeah.

Robert Hess: What about the whole notion of it being more of a service oriented sort of thing, so I'm writing more of an almost non-GUI application and running on a server, and I'm going to be attacking it with a web client, and coming at it and asking for responses to track a package or something like that. Does that change the mindset at all, or is that still just the same service-side orientation?

Anders Hejlsberg: Well, I think it, in a sense, makes you think a little bit more about abstractions in your applications. You would tend to think more about, how do I layer my application into a business logic tier and a presentation tier, how do I put APIs on my business logic such that it can either be used by my presentation logic to present HTML or a client based UI, or even just be direct entry points for web services that go over the Web. So, there's, you know, you tend to think about that a little bit more, so as I said earlier, you're not just writing these monolithical things anymore.

Robert Hess: Do you see this as lending itself more towards people using other people's components a lot easier than they have today? I remember when I used to work at Boeing, we had this big thing going on about code reuse. We had to take and make sure that any application we wrote, any code we wrote was specifically designed for code reuse, and while in thought it sounded like a great idea, in practice, it never quite ended up being utilized that well, because it's just really hard to reuse someone else's code. Do you think this might actually enable that better?

Anders Hejlsberg: I think it will, I think that the thing, the key operative here is actually, for that, is the .NET Framework. It is the fact that we have defined this substrate upon which you can build components. And we say a lot, you know, about how you put them into classes, how you make them components, you know, we give you strong decide guidelines and indeed the whole framework serves as an example of that, but key to it is that it is uniformly accessible from a variety of programming languages, so the problem you've talked about here, for example, if some guy's writing some language or some library in Cobol and you want to use it from C++, you know, it's going to be very hard.

We're actually giving you a substrate that allows you to do that kind of interoperability. So you definitely stand a much better chance of having your components interoperate. Because, in reality, the thing that's often hard for people is that components are written with different design philosophies or at different abstraction levels, and that's what confuses people. They are not accustomed to this style of API, and so they get lost in the infrastructure, they can't see the forest for the trees, if you know what I mean. And so by saying a lot about how you write components, and giving you a consistently available API and infrastructure for writing these components, you stand a much better chance of getting better reusability.

Robert Hess: Well, I think that sounds like a pretty good explanation, are there any final closing words you think are important for an audience to understand in order to grasp the architectural importance of C# as a language?

Anders Hejlsberg: Well I think the best way to do that is to play with it yourself. So, I would urge people to download it from our site, and I'm sure you could give them the address. Download it, play with it, write some examples, join our user groups or newsgroups, talk to other people that have used it, you know, see what their experience is on. I think you'll have a good time.

C#: A Message Queuing Application

This article by Carl Nolan, who works for the Western Region of the Microsoft E-Commerce Solutions Team, was published in fall 2000 on MSDN Online. A recent article presented a solution for a highly available message queuing scalable load-balancing solution architecture. This solution entailed the development of a Windows service that acted as a smart message router. Up to now, such a solution was the realm of the Microsoft Visual C++ programmer. With the advent of the.NET Framework, this is no longer the case. The solution is now possible in a simple object-oriented program. To prove this, Nolan outlines a Windows service solution designed to process several message queues, focusing on the application of the .NET Framework and C#.

Introduction

Microsoft recently introduced a new platform for building integrated applications—the Microsoft .NET Framework. The .NET Framework allows developers to quickly build and deploy Web Services and applications in any programming language. This language-neutral framework is made possible by the Microsoft Intermediate Language (MSIL) and just-in-time (JIT) compiler.

Along with the .NET Framework has come a new programming language, C# (pronounced "C sharp"). C# is a simple, modern, object-oriented, and type-safe programming language. Utilizing the .NET Framework and C# (in addition to Microsoft® Visual Basic® and Managed C++), one can write highly functional Microsoft Windows® and Web applications and services. This article presents such a solution, focusing on the application of the .NET Framework and C# rather than the programming language. A C# language introduction can be found in the C# Introduction and Overview.

The recent article, MSMQ: A Scalable, Highly Available Load-Balancing Solution, presented a solution for a highly available Message Queuing (MSMQ) scalable load-balancing solution architecture. This solution involved the development of a Windows service that acted as a smart message router. Previously, such a solution was the realm of the Microsoft Visual C++® programmer. With the advent of the .NET Framework this is no longer the case, as the following solution will show.

The .NET Framework Application

The solution to be outlined is a Windows service designed to process several message queues; each is processed by multiple threads, receiving and processing messages. Sample processes are included for routing messages using a round-robin technique or an application-specific value (the message **AppSpecific** property) from a list of destination queues, and for calling a component method with the message properties. In the latter case the requirement of the component is that it implements a given interface, called IWebMessage. To handle errors the application will send messages that cannot be processed into an error queue.

The messaging application is structured similarly to the previous Active Template Library (ATL) application, the main differences being the encapsulation of the code to manage the service and the use of the .NET Framework components. Because the .NET Framework is object-oriented, it should come as no surprise that all one has to do to create a Windows service is create a class that inherits from **ServiceBase**, from the System.ServiceControl assembly.

Application Structure

The main class in the application is **ServiceControl**, the class that inherits from **ServiceBase**. With inheritance from **ServiceBase** one must implement **OnStart** and **OnStop** methods, in addition to the optional **OnPause** and **OnContinue** methods. The class is actually constructed within the static method, **Main**:

```
using System;
using System.ServiceProcess;

public class ServiceControl: ServiceBase
{
   // main entry point that creates the service object
   public static void Main()
   {
      ServiceBase.Run(new ServiceControl());
   }

   // constructor object that defines the service parameters
   public ServiceControl()
   {
      CanPauseAndContinue = true;
      ServiceName = "MSDNMessageService";
      AutoLog = false;
   }
```

```
    protected override void OnStart(string[] args) {...}
    protected override void OnStop() {...}
    protected override void OnPause() {...}
    protected override void OnContinue() {...}
}
```

The **ServiceControl** class creates a series of **CWorker** objects, an instance of a **CWorker** class being created for each message queue requiring processing. The **CWorker** class in turn creates a series of **CWorkerThread** objects, based on the required number of threads defined to process the queue. The **CWorkerThread** class creates a processing thread that will perform the actual service work.

The main purpose of the **CWorker** and **CWorkerThread** classes is the acknowledgment of the Service control Start, Stop, Pause, and Continue commands. Because these processes must be nonblocking, the command actions will ultimately exact an action on a background processing thread.

The **CWorkerThread** is an abstract class that is inherited by **CWorkerThreadAppSpecific**, **CWorkerThreadRoundRobin**, and **CWorkerThreadAssembly**. Each of these classes processes messages in a different manner. The first two process a message by sending it to another queue (the difference being the manner in which the receiving queue path is determined), the latter using the message properties to call a component method.

Error handling within the .NET Framework is based around a base **Exception** class. When ones throws or catches errors, they must be of a class derived from **Exception**. The **CWorkerThreadException** class is such an implementation, extending the base class with the addition of a property that defines whether the service should continue running.

Finally, the application contains two structs. These value types define the run-time parameters of a worker process or thread, in order to simplify the construction of the **CWorker** and **CWorkerThread** objects. The use of a value-type struct rather than a reference-type class ensures that values rather than references are maintained to these run-time parameters.

IWebMessage interface

One of the provided **CWorkerThread** implementations is a class that calls a component method. This class, called **CWorkerThreadAssembly**, uses the IWebMessage interface to define the contract between the service and the component.

Unlike the current version of Microsoft Visual Studio®, C# interfaces can be explicitly defined in any language, removing the need to create and compile IDL files. Use of the C# IWebMessage interface is defined as follows:

```
public interface IWebMessage
{
    WebMessageReturn Process(string sMessageLabel, string sMessageBody, int
iAppSpecific);
    void Release();
}
```

The **Process** method, as in the ATL code, is designated for processing messages. The return code of the **Process** method is defined as the enumeration type **WebMessageReturn**:

```
public enum WebMessageReturn
{
    ReturnGood,
    ReturnBad,
    ReturnAbort
}
```

The enumeration definitions are as follows: Good continues processing, Bad writes the message to the error queue, and Abort terminates processing. The **Release** method provides a mechanism for the service to gracefully destroy the class instance. Because the destructor of the instance of the class is only called during garbage collection, it is a good practice to ensure that all classes that have expensive resources (such as database connections) have a method that can be called, prior to destruction, to release these resources.

Namespaces

At this point, a brief mention of namespaces is warranted. Namespaces allow applications to be organized into logical elements, for both internal and external representation. All the code within this service is contained within the MSDNMessageService.Service namespace. Although the service code is contained within several files, because they are contained within the same namespace, you do not need to reference the other files.

As the IWebMessage interface is contained within the MSDNMessageService.Interface namespace, the thread class that uses this interface has an interface namespace import.

Service Classes

The purpose of the application is to monitor and process message queues, each queue having a different process to be performed on received messages. The application is implemented as a Windows service.

The ServiceBase class

As mentioned before, the basic structure of a service is a class that inherits from **ServiceBase**. The important methods are **OnStart**, **OnStop**, **OnPause**, and **OnContinue**, with each overridden method corresponding directly to a Service control action. The purpose of the **OnStart** method is to create **CWorker** objects, the **CWorker** class in turn creating **CWorkerThread** objects from which the threads that perform the service work are created.

The run-time configuration of the service, and thus the properties of the **CWorker** and **CWorkerThread** objects, is maintained within an XML-based configuration file, named after the created .exe file, but with a .cfg suffix. An example configuration would be:

```xml
<?xml version="1.0"?>
<configuration>
<ProcessList>
  <ProcessDefinition
        ProcessName="Worker1"
        ProcessDesc="Message Worker with 2 Threads"
        ProcessType="AppSpecific"
        ProcessThreads="2"
        InputQueue=".\private$\test_load1"
        ErrorQueue=".\private$\test_error">
    <OutputList>
      <OutputDefinition OutputName=".\private$\test_out11" />
      <OutputDefinition OutputName=".\private$\test_out12" />
    </OutputList>
  </ProcessDefinition>
  <ProcessDefinition
        ProcessName="Worker2"
        ProcessDesc="Assembly Worker with 1 Thread"
        ProcessType="Assembly"
        ProcessThreads="1"
        InputQueue=".\private$\test_load2"
        ErrorQueue=".\private$\test_error">
    <OutputList>
      <OutputDefinition OutputName="C:\MSDNMessageService\MessageExample.dll" />
      <OutputDefinition
OutputName="MSDNMessageService.MessageSample.ExampleClass" />
    </OutputList>
  </ProcessDefinition>
</ProcessList>
</configuration>
```

Access to this information is managed through the **ConfigManager** class, from the System.Configuration assembly. The static **Get** method returns a collection of information, which can then be enumerated through to obtain the individual properties. These sets of properties determine the run-time characteristics of a worker object.

In addition to this configuration file, you should create a metafile defining the structure of the XML file, with a reference to the metafile placed in the servers machine.cfg configuration file:

```xml
<?xml version ="1.0"?>
<MetaData xmlns="x-schema:CatMeta.xms">
   <DatabaseMeta InternalName="MessageService">
   <ServerWiring Interceptor="Core_XMLInterceptor"/>
   <Collection
         InternalName="Process" PublicName="ProcessList"
         PublicRowName="ProcessDefinition"
         SchemaGeneratorFlags="EMITXMLSCHEMA">
     <Property InternalName="ProcessName" Type="String" MetaFlags="PRIMARYKEY"
/>
     <Property InternalName="ProcessDesc" Type="String" />
     <Property InternalName="ProcessType" Type="Int32" DefaultValue="RoundRobin"
>
        <Enum InternalName="RoundRobin"  Value="0"/>
        <Enum InternalName="AppSpecific" Value="1"/>
        <Enum InternalName="Assembly" Value="2"/>
     </Property>
     <Property InternalName="ProcessThreads" Type="Int32" DefaultValue="1" />
     <Property InternalName="InputQueue" Type="String" />
     <Property InternalName="ErrorQueue" Type="String" />
     <Property InternalName="OutputName" Type="String" />
     <QueryMeta InternalName="All" MetaFlags="ALL" />
     <QueryMeta InternalName="QueryByFile" CellName="__FILE" Operator="EQUAL"
/>
   </Collection>
   <Collection
         InternalName="Output" PublicName="OutputList"
         PublicRowName="OutputDefinition"
         SchemaGeneratorFlags="EMITXMLSCHEMA">
     <Property InternalName="ProcessName" Type="String" MetaFlags="PRIMARYKEY"
/>
     <Property InternalName="OutputName" Type="String" MetaFlags="PRIMARYKEY" />
     <QueryMeta InternalName="All" MetaFlags="ALL" />
     <QueryMeta InternalName="QueryByFile" CellName="__FILE" Operator="EQUAL"
/>
```

```
    </Collection>
    </DatabaseMeta>
    <RelationMeta
        PrimaryTable="Process" PrimaryColumns="ProcessName"
        ForeignTable="Output"  ForeignColumns="ProcessName"
        MetaFlags="USECONTAINMENT"/>
</MetaData>
```

As the **Service** class must maintain a list of created worker objects, the Hashtable collection is used, holding a list of name/value pairs of type object. The Hashtable allows for querying values by key, in addition to supporting enumerations. In the application, the XML process name is the unique key:

```csharp
private Hashtable htWorkers = new Hashtable();
IConfigCollection cWorkers = ConfigManager.Get("ProcessList", new
AppDomainSelector());
foreach (IConfigItem ciWorker in cWorkers)
{
    WorkerFormatter sfWorker = new WorkerFormatter();
    sfWorker.ProcessName = (string)ciWorker["ProcessName"];
    sfWorker.ProcessDesc = (string)ciWorker["ProcessDesc"];
    sfWorker.NumberThreads = (int)ciWorker["ProcessThreads"];
    sfWorker.InputQueue = (string)ciWorker["InputQueue"];
    sfWorker.ErrorQueue = (string)ciWorker["ErrorQueue"];
    // calculate and define the processing type
    switch ((int)ciWorker["ProcessType"])
    {
        case 0:
            sfWorker.ProcessType = WorkerFormatter.SFProcessType.ProcessRoundRobin;
            break;
        case 1:
            sfWorker.ProcessType = WorkerFormatter.SFProcessType.ProcessAppSpecific;
            break;
        case 2:
            sfWorker.ProcessType = WorkerFormatter.SFProcessType.ProcessAssembly;
            break;
        default:
            throw new Exception("Unknown Processing Type");
    }
    // perform more work to read output informaiton
    string sProcessName = (string)ciWorker["ProcessName"];
    if (htWorkers.ContainsKey(sProcessName))
        throw new ArgumentException("Process Name Must be Unique: " +
sProcessName);
    htWorkers.Add(sProcessName, new CWorker(sfWorker));
}
```

The main piece of information missing from the code is the acquisition of the output data. Within each Process Definition there is a set of corresponding Output Definition entries. This information is read via a simple query:

```
string sQuery = "SELECT * FROM OutputList WHERE ProcessName=" +
    sfWorker.ProcessName + " AND Selector=appdomain://";
ConfigQuery qQuery = new ConfigQuery(sQuery);
IConfigCollection cOutputs = ConfigManager.Get("OutputList", qQuery);
int iSize = cOutputs.Count, iLoop = 0;
sfWorker.OutputName = new string[iSize];
foreach (IConfigItem ciOutput in cOutputs)
    sfWorker.OutputName[iLoop++] = (string)ciOutput["OutputName"];
```

Both the **CWorkerThread** and the **Cworker** classes have corresponding service control methods that are called according to the service control action. As each **CWorker** object is referenced in the Hashtable, the contents of the Hashtable are enumerated, in order to call the appropriate service control method:

```
foreach (CWorker cWorker in htWorkers.Values)
    cWorker.Start();
```

Similarly, the implemented **OnPause**, **OnContinue**, and **OnStop** methods operate by calling the corresponding methods on the **CWorker** objects.

The CWorker class

The primary function of the **CWorker** class is to create and manage **CWorkerThread** objects. The **Start**, **Stop**, **Pause**, and **Continue** methods call the corresponding **CWorkerThread** methods. The actual **CWorkerThread** objects are created in the **Start** method. Like the **Service** class, which uses a Hashtable to manage the references to the worker objects, **CWorker** uses an ArrayList, a simple dynamically sized array, to maintain a list of thread objects.

Within this array the **CWorker** class creates one of the implemented versions of the **CWorkerThread** class. The **CWorkerThread** class, discussed next, is an abstract class that must be inherited. The derived classes define how a message is to be processed:

```
aThreads = new ArrayList();
for (int idx=0; idx<sfWorker.NumberThreads; idx++)
{
    WorkerThreadFormatter wfThread = new WorkerThreadFormatter();
    wfThread.ProcessName = sfWorker.ProcessName;
    wfThread.ProcessDesc = sfWorker.ProcessDesc;
    wfThread.ThreadNumber = idx;
    wfThread.InputQueue = sfWorker.InputQueue;
    wfThread.ErrorQueue = sfWorker.ErrorQueue;
    wfThread.OutputName = sfWorker.OutputName;
    // define the worker type and insert into the work thread struct
    CWorkerThread wtBase;
```

```
switch (sfWorker.ProcessType)
{
    case WorkerFormatter.SFProcessType.ProcessRoundRobin:
        wtBase = new CWorkerThreadRoundRobin(this, wfThread);
        break;
    case WorkerFormatter.SFProcessType.ProcessAppSpecific:
        wtBase = new CWorkerThreadAppSpecific(this, wfThread);
        break;
    case WorkerFormatter.SFProcessType.ProcessAssembly:
        wtBase = new CWorkerThreadAssembly(this, wfThread);
        break;
    default:
        throw new Exception("Unknown Processing Type");
}
// add the calls to the array
aThreads.Insert(idx, wtBase);
}
```

Once all the objects have been created, they can be started by calling the **Start** method of each thread object:

```
foreach(CWorkerThread cThread in aThreads)
    cThread.Start();
```

The **Stop**, **Pause**, and **Continue** methods all perform similar operations within a foreach loop. The **Stop** method does have the following garbage collection operation:

```
GC.SuppressFinalize(this);
```

Within the class destructor, the **Stop** method gets called, which allows the objects to be correctly terminated if the **Stop** method is not explicitly called. If the **Stop** method is called, the destructor is not needed. The **SuppressFinalize** method prevents the object's **Finalize** method, the actual implementation of the destructor, from being called.

The CWorkerThread abstract class

The **CWorkerThread** is an abstract class that is inherited by **CWorkerThreadAppSpecifc**, **CWorkerThreadRoundRobin**, and **CWorkerThreadAssembly**. Because most of the processing of a queue is identical, regardless of how the message gets processed, the **CWorkerThread** class provides this functionality. The class provides abstract methods that must be overridden to manage resources and process messages.

The work of the class is once again implemented in the **Start**, **Stop**, **Pause**, and **Continue** methods. The input and error queues are referenced in the **Start** method. Within the .NET Framework, messaging is handled by the System.Messaging namespace:

```
// try to open the queue and set the default read and write properties
MessageQueue mqInput = new MessageQueue(sInputQueue);
mqInput.MessageReadPropertyFilter.Body = true;
mqInput.MessageReadPropertyFilter.AppSpecific = true;
MessageQueue mqError = new MessageQueue(sErrorQueue);
// set the formatter to be activex if using MSMQ COM
mqInput.Formatter = new ActiveXMessageFormatter();
mqError.Formatter = new ActiveXMessageFormatter();
```

Once the message queue references are defined, a thread is created for the actual processing function, called **ProcessMessages**. Within the .NET Framework, threading is easily accomplished using the System.Threading namespace:

```
procMessage = new Thread(new ThreadStart(ProcessMessages));
procMessage.Start();
```

The **ProcessMessages** function is a processing loop based on a Boolean value. When the value is set to false, the process loop terminates. Thus, the **Stop** method of the thread object merely sets this Boolean value and then joins the thread with the main thread, in addition to closing the open message queues:

```
// join the service thread and the processing thread
bRun = false;
procMessage.Join();
// close the open message queues
mqInput.Close();
mqError.Close();
```

The **Pause** method merely sets a Boolean value that causes the processing thread to sleep for half a second:

```
if (bPause)
   Thread.Sleep(500);
```

Finally, each of the **Start**, **Stop**, **Pause**, and **Continue** methods call abstract **OnStart**, **OnStop**, **OnPause**, and **OnContinue** methods. These abstract methods provide the hooks for implemented classes to capture and release required resources.

The **ProcessMessages** loop has the following basic structure:

- Receive a **Message**.
- If a **Message** has a successful **Receive**, call the abstract **ProcessMessage** method.
- If the **Receive** or **ProcessMessage** fails, send the **Message** into an error queue.

```csharp
Message mInput;
try
{
   // read from the queue with a wait of 1 second
   mInput = mqInput.Receive(new TimeSpan(0,0,0,1));
}
catch (MessageQueueException mqe)
{
   // set the message to null as not to be processed
   mInput = null;
   // look at the error code and see if there was a timeout
   if (mqe.ErrorCode != (-1072824293) ) //0xC00E001B
   {
      // if not a timeout throw an error and log the error number
      LogError("Error : " + mqe.Message);
      throw mqe;
   }
}
if (mInput != null)
{
   // have a message to process, call the process message abstract method
   try
   {
      ProcessMessage(mInput);
   }
   // catch error thrown where exception status known
   catch (CWorkerThreadException ex)
   {
      ProcessError(mInput, ex.Terminate);
   }
   // catch an unknown exception and call terminate
   catch
   {
      ProcessError(mInput, true);
   }
}
```

The **ProcessError** method sends the erroneous message to the error queue. In addition, it might throw an exception to abnormally terminate the thread. It would perform this action if a terminate error, or type **CWorkerThreadException**, were thrown by the **ProcessMessage** method.

The CworkerThread-derived classes

Any class that inherits from **CWorkerThread** must provide **OnStart**, **OnStop**, **OnPause**, **OnContinue**, and **ProcessMessage** methods. The **OnStart** and **OnStop** methods acquire and release processing resources. The **OnPause** and **OnContinue** methods allow the temporary release and reacquisition of these resources. The **ProcessMessage** method should process a message, throwing a **CWorkerThreadException** exception in the event of a failure.

As the **CWorkerThread** constructor defines run-time parameters, the derived classes must call the base class constructor:

```
public CWorkerThreadDerived(CWorker v_cParent, WorkerThreadFormatter v_wfThread)
    : base (v_cParent, v_wfThread) {}
```

Derived classes are provided for two types of processing: sending messages to another queue or calling a component method. The two implementations that receive and send messages use a round-robin technique or an application offset, held in the message **AppSpecific** property, as the determining factor for which queue to use. The configuration file in this scenario should contain a list of queue paths. The implemented **OnStart** and **OnStop** methods should open and close a reference to these queues:

```
iQueues = wfThread.OutputName.Length;
mqOutput = new MessageQueue[iQueues];
for (int idx=0; idx<iQueues; idx++)
{
    mqOutput[idx] = new MessageQueue(wfThread.OutputName[idx]);
    mqOutput[idx].Formatter = new ActiveXMessageFormatter();
}
```

In these scenarios, processing the message is simple: Send the message to the required output queue. In a round-robin situation, the process would be:

```
try
{
    mqOutput[iNextQueue].Send(v_mInput);
}
catch (Exception ex)
{
    // if an error force terminate exception
    throw new CWorkerThreadException(ex.Message, true);
}
// calculate the next queue number
iNextQueue++;
iNextQueue %= iQueues;
```

The latter implementation, calling a component with the message parameters, is a little more interesting. Using the IWebMessage interface, the **ProcessMessage** method calls into a .NET component. The **OnStart** and **OnStop** methods obtain and release a reference to this component.

The configuration file in this scenario should contain two items: the full class name and the location of the file in which the class resides. The **Process** method is called on the component as defined in the IWebMessage interface.

To obtain the object reference, the **Activator.CreateInstance** method is used. The function requires an Assembly Type, in this case derived from the assembly file path and class name. Once an object reference is obtained it is cast into the appropriate interface:

```
private IWebMessage iwmSample;
private string sFilePath, sTypeName;
// save the assembly path and type name
sFilePath = wfThread.OutputName[0];
sTypeName = wfThread.OutputName[1];
// obtain a reference to the required object
Assembly asmSample = Assembly.LoadFrom(sFilePath);
Type typSample = asmSample.GetType(sTypeName);
object objSample = Activator.CreateInstance(typSample);
// cast to the required interface on the object
iwmSample = (IWebMessage)objSample;
```

When an object reference is obtained, the **ProcessMessage** method calls the **Process** method on the IWebMessage Interface:

```
WebMessageReturn wbrSample;
try
{
    // define the parameters for the method call
    string sLabel = v_mInput.Label;
    string sBody = (string)v_mInput.Body;
    int iAppSpecific = v_mInput.AppSpecific;
    // call the method and catch the return code
    wbrSample = iwmSample.Process(sLabel, sBody, iAppSpecific);
}
catch (InvalidCastException ex)
{
    // if an error in casting message details then force a nonterminate exception
    throw new CWorkerThreadException(ex.Message, false);
}
catch (Exception ex)
```

(continued)

(continued)

```
{
    // if an error calling the assembly then force an terminate exception
    throw new CWorkerThreadException(ex.Message, true);
}
// if no error review the return status of the object call
switch (wbrSample)
{
    case WebMessageReturn.ReturnBad:
        throw new CWorkerThreadException
            .("Unable to process message: Message marked bad", false);
    case WebMessageReturn.ReturnAbort:
        throw new CWorkerThreadException
            ("Unable to process message: Process terminating", true);
    default:
        break;
}
```

The example component provided writes the message body into a database table. In this case you might want to abort processing if a severe database error is captured, but merely mark the message as erroneous otherwise.

Because the instance of the class created for this example might acquire and hold expensive database resources, the **OnPause** and **OnContinue** methods release and reacquire the object reference.

Instrumentation

As in all good applications, instrumentation is provided to monitor the status of the application. The .NET Framework has greatly simplified inclusion of event logging, performance counters, and Windows Management Instrumentation (WMI) into applications. The messaging application uses event logging and performance counters, both from the System.Diagnostics assembly.

Within the **ServiceBase** class you can enable automatic event logging. In addition, the ServiceBase **EventLog** member supports writing to the Application event log:

```
EventLog.WriteEntry(sMyMessage, EventLogEntryType.Information);
```

For an application to write to event logs other than the Application log, it can easily create and obtain a reference to an **EventLog** source, as is done in the **CWorker** class, and can use the **WriteEntry** method for recording log entries:

```
private EventLog cLog;
string sSource = ServiceControl.ServiceControlName;
string sLog = "Application";
// see if the source exists creating if not
if (!EventLog.SourceExists(sSource))
```

```
   EventLog.CreateEventSource(sSource, sLog);
// create the log object and reference the now defined source
cLog = new EventLog();
cLog.Source = sSource;
// write an entry to inform successful creation
cLog.WriteEntry("Successfully Created", EventLogEntryType.Information);
```

Performance counters have been greatly simplified by the .NET Framework. This messaging application provides counters that track the number and number per second of messages processed, for each processing thread; the worker from which threads derive; and the application as a whole. To provide this functionality, you have to define the performance counter categories, and then increment corresponding counter instances.

Within the Service **OnStart** method performance counter categories are defined. These categories represent the two counters, total messages, and messages processed per second:

```
CounterCreationData[] cdMessage = new CounterCreationData[2];
cdMessage[0] = new CounterCreationData("Messages/Total", "Total Messages
Processed",
PerformanceCounterType.NumberOfItems64);
cdMessage[1] = new CounterCreationData("Messages/Second", "Messages Processed a
Second",
PerformanceCounterType.RateOfChangePerSecond32);
PerformanceCounterCategory.Create("MSDN Message Service", "MSDN Message Service
Counters", cdMessage);
```

Once the performance counter categories are defined, a **PerformanceCounter** object is created to provide access to counter instance functionality. The **PerformanceCounter** object requires the Category and Counter name and an optional Instance name. For the worker process, using the process name from the XML file, the code is as follows:

```
pcMsgTotWorker = new PerformanceCounter("MSDN Message Service", "Messages/Total",
sProcessName);
pcMsgSecWorker = new PerformanceCounter("MSDN Message Service",
"Messages/Second", sProcessName);
pcMsgTotWorker.RawValue = 0;
pcMsgSecWorker.RawValue = 0;
```

Incrementing the counters is then simply a matter of calling the appropriate method:

```
pcMsgTotWorker.IncrementBy(1);
pcMsgSecWorker.IncrementBy(1);
```

On a final note, when the service is stopped the installed performance counter category should be deleted from the system:

```
PerformanceCounterCategory.Delete("MSDN Message Service");
```

For performance counters to work within the .NET Framework a special service needs to be running. This service, **PerfCounterService**, provides the shared memory to which the counter information is written and is then read by the performance counter system.

Installation

Before we finish, a brief mention is warranted about installation and an installation utility called installutil.exe. Because this application is a Windows service, it must be installed using installutil.exe. To facilitate this, a class is required that inherits the **Installer** class from the System.Configuration.Install assembly:

```
public class ServiceRegister: Installer
{
    private ServiceInstaller serviceInstaller;
    private ServiceProcessInstaller processInstaller;
    public ServiceRegister()
    {
        // create the service installer
        serviceInstaller = new ServiceInstaller();
        serviceInstaller.StartType = ServiceStart.Manual;
        serviceInstaller.ServiceName = ServiceControl.ServiceControlName;
        serviceInstaller.DisplayName = ServiceControl.ServiceControlDesc;
        Installers.Add(serviceInstaller);
        // create the process installer
        processInstaller = new ServiceProcessInstaller();
        processInstaller.RunUnderSystemAccount = true;
        Installers.Add(processInstaller);
    }
}
```

As this sample class shows, for a Windows service, an installer is required for the service and another for the service process, to define the account under which the service will run. Other installers allow for registration of resources such as event logs and performance counters.

Conclusion

As one can see from this sample .NET Framework application, what was previously only in the realm of Visual C++ programmers is now possible in a simple object-oriented program. Although this article focuses on C#, everything written here can also be written in Visual Basic and Managed C++. The new .NET Framework has enabled developers to create highly functional, scalable Windows applications and services from any programming language.

Not only has the new .NET Framework simplified and extended the programming possibilities, often-forgotten application instrumentation, such as performance monitor counters and event log notifications, can be easily incorporated into applications. This also applies to Windows Management Instrumentation (WMI), although that is not used in this application.

Introducing JScript.NET

This article by Andrew Clinick, a program manager in the Microsoft Script Technology Group, was published in summer 2000 on MSDN Online. JScript.NET is a major evolution of JScript and the scripting platform. It provides a rich, robust language that builds on the existing script language while providing a flexible way to start building bigger scripts. The key to all of these improvements in JScript and Visual Basic is the .NET Framework on which they are built. This framework provides even more scriptable objects for developers to use in their solutions. It also extends the capabilities of developers' scripts to allow almost anything to be scripted on their machines or on the Internet.

This week marks a major step forward for script with the first public showing of JScript.NET and Visual Basic.NET at the Professional Developers Conference (PDC) in Orlando, and the release of Windows Script version 5.5 (available for download). I thought I'd take this opportunity to go over some of the key advances in JScript® and Visual Basic® Scripting Edition (VBScript), and how scripting in general will evolve to take advantage of the new .NET platform.

What About VBScript?

Whenever I talk about JScript.NET, I always hear questions about VBScript and where that fits into the new .NET scripting plans. Since VBScript's inception a little over four years ago, we've been getting requests to add Visual Basic functions to VBScript, and to allow people to use "real" Visual Basic where they would traditionally use VBScript. The VBScript language has made considerable improvements in versions 5.0 and 5.5, so when we sat down to look at what we could add to VBScript, it became apparent that we'd eventually have to add pretty much all of Visual Basic's features. To achieve this (and, hopefully, to keep VBScript users happy), we could either re-implement Visual Basic ourselves, or work with the Visual Basic team to make Visual Basic a script engine. We chose the latter, because it would guarantee that the languages would remain in synch, and that VBScript would gain a slew of new features, such as finally being able to call *any* object, and not just automation (**IDispatch**) objects.

One caveat to this merging of the two languages is that a small number of VBScript features—such as **Eval** and the **Execute** functions—are not available in the first release of Visual Basic.NET. Although it may seem like we've thrown the baby out with the bathwater here, and destroyed the notion of Visual Basic.NET as a "dynamic" scripting language, that's not really the case. The first release of Visual Basic.NET is targeted at building Web services and applications, using ASP+ on the server—where hopefully you aren't using functions such as **Eval** or **ExecuteGlobal**. We intend to add these features back into the Visual Basic.NET language in the next release, in time for our integration with Microsoft Internet Explorer (where the dynamic features of the language are more useful). An added bonus is that adding **Eval** to Visual Basic.NET for Internet Explorer also means adding **Eval** to Visual Basic.NET for your other .NET applications, because it's the same language.

The new features in Visual Basic are thoroughly documented on MSDN. Rather than re-iterate what is already covered there, I'm going to focus this article on the new features in JScript. The key thing to remember is that, from now on, there will be just one Visual Basic language to learn—which, we hope, will make your life as a .NET developer even easier. We'd love to get your feedback on this, so please feel free to use the scripting newsgroups or to e-mail us at msscript@microsoft.com.

JScript.NET

This is probably the biggest leap in functionality for JScript since the 1996 introduction of JScript version 1.0 with Internet Explorer 3.0. JScript has traditionally been used to develop client-side scripts due to its ubiquitous, cross-platform support on the Internet, but we've been seeing a steady increase in the usage of JScript on the server—particularly in Active Server Pages (ASP). For example, your favorite Web site (MSDN) uses a large amount of server-side JScript, as do many other sites on the Internet.

Using JScript on the server has resulted in people asking for performance improvements—you can never have too much performance on the server. However, now is a good time to point out that both the traditional JScript and VBScript languages, and the new Visual Basic.NET and JScript.NET languages, have very similar performance characteristics: Neither is noticeably faster than the other in the general case.

As scripts get bigger, script authors need to be able to write more robust code. And as programs become more complex, script authors have become frustrated by JScript's limitation of only dealing with automation (**IDispatch**) objects.

JScript.NET was designed with these requirements in mind. The JScript team was keen to ensure that the new language features were added in an evolutionary manner, so that you can leverage your existing JScript skills in the .NET world. It was vital that JScript.NET feel like a new version of the existing language, rather than a completely new language.

Evolution

The key part of JScript's evolution is keeping the language recognizably JScript, so that it will run existing JScript code and that any enhancements will work within the existing language definitions. For example, one of the new features is the introduction of types to the language. Types in JScript.NET are an extension of the existing variable and function declaration mechanisms, and are entirely optional. One of the defining qualities of a script language is the ability to write code without having to worry about the types of variables—or having to worry about variables at all, for that matter. Making types optional allows developers to leverage their existing JScript skills and source code, while providing a smooth migration path for adding types to new and existing programs to reap the benefits of improved performance and robustness.

Working closely with ECMA

Jscript's association with the ECMAScript standard has helped its success considerably. The standard has allowed innovation in the language to be developed in conjunction with all the members of the ECMAScript Technical Committee—which means that both JScript and JavaScript have remained very compatible throughout, and any new features are discussed and designed together. This approach ensures that both languages can benefit from the ideas of many companies, instead of being isolated developments within individual companies.

The development of JScript.NET has continued this partnership, so that all the new features have been designed in conjunction with other ECMA members. It's important to note that the language features in the JScript.NET PDC release are not final. We're working with other ECMA members to finalize the design as soon as possible. In fact, there's an ECMA meeting this week at the PDC where we'll try to sort out some of the remaining issues.

Performance

Enough of the touchy, feely features of JScript.NET. Let's get into some of the real features, and how they will make a difference to your development. Perhaps the most important feature area of JScript.NET is the performance improvements to the language. The most dramatic impact on performance in JScript.NET is that it is a true compiled language, which makes it possible to achieve performance comparable to that of C# and Visual Basic.NET. From a language perspective, the key mechanism for getting performance improvements in JScript is the addition of types to the language. Typing in JScript.NET has been introduced via both traditional (explicit) type declarations, and implicit type inferencing. Type inferencing is an exciting technology that analyzes your use of variables in a script and infers the type of the variable for you. This means that you can get considerable improvements in speed using existing scripts without having to type your variables.

For example, consider the following JScript program:

```
function test()
{

    for (var x = 0; x < 100; x++)
    {
        print(x);
    }
}
```

When JScript.NET compiles this program, it analyzes the use of x and determines that x is only ever used to hold numeric values. As a result, x can safely be defined as a number. This provides a performance improvement, since the JScript compiler can optimize the use of x as a number rather than as a generic **Object** (or variant) that could potentially contain any type of value.

In order to exploit the type inferencing ability of the JScript compiler, you need to follow a few simple rules. Luckily, these rules are also part of general good coding practices, so you may already be following these rules in your existing code. The three simple rules to follow are:

1. Always declare your local variables. This may sound like an obvious point, but it is important. JScript can infer the types of local (function) variables only, not global variables. If you implicitly declare a variable (use it without declaring it in a **var** statement) it becomes a global variable, and can't be optimized.
2. Only use a variable for one type of data. If you declare a variable and use it to store a number, don't re-use the same variable later to store a string or another type of data. If you do this, JScript has no choice but to make the variable a generic **Object** (variant).

Here are some examples of how to follow these simple rules:

```
// can't infer the type -- glob is a global
var glob = 42;

function myfunc()
{
    // can't infer the type -- s is not declared so it is
    // created as a global
    s = "hello";
```

```
    // type inferencing works here -- i is declared
    var i = 0;

    // can't infer the type -- q is assigned different data types
    var q = new Date();
    q = 3.14159;
}
```

Type inferencing is a great technology, but it has two drawbacks. First, it always errs on the side of caution. Second, while type inferencing provides performance improvements, it won't help you catch type mismatch errors or other programming errors. To overcome this, JScript.NET provides a way to explicitly declare a variable as being of a particular type. This is achieved by using the new type annotation syntax on the **var** statement and for function parameter lists and return types. Type annotations are achieved by adding a colon (:) to the variable, parameter, or function declaration, followed by the type name.

For example:

```
// Declare an integer variable.
var myInt : int = 42;

// Declare a function that returns a String
function GetName() : String
{
    // function code
}

// Declare a function that takes a double parameter
// and returns a Boolean
function CheckNumber(dVal : double) : Boolean
{
    // function code
}
```

I converted the weather conditions function from my Scripting Web Services article to demonstrate adding type annotations to a function. The function takes a single String parameter, **strCity**, and returns a String result. Providing the type annotations allow the JScript.NET compiler to both optimize the compiled version of the function, and to provide compile-time type checking whenever the function is called (this also works from other languages, such as C# and Visual Basic). The key here is that adding type annotations is optional, but the benefits are considerable—so I encourage you to use them as much as possible.

```
function getConditions(strCity : String) : String
{
   var now : Date = new Date();
   switch (strCity.toUpperCase())
   {
   case "LONDON":
      if (now.getMonth() <= 7 || now.getMonth() >= 9)
      {
         return "overcast";
      }
      else
      {
         return "partly overcast and humid";
      }
      break;

   case "SEATTLE":
      if (now.getMonth() == 7 && now.getDay() == 4)
      {
         return "torrential rain";
      }
      else
      {
         return "rain";
      }
      break;

   case "LA":
      return "smoggy";
      break;

   case "PHOENIX":
      return "damn hot";
      break;

   default:
      return "partly cloudy with a chance of showers";
   }
}
```

In JScript.NET, you can also declare variables using any .NET Framework type. Additional types can be introduced into JScript either by importing a namespace that contains the new type, or by declaring user-defined types as classes. There is potential overlap between .NET Framework types and JScript built-in objects, so JScript.NET provides a mapping between the two for type annotations:

Boolean	.NET Framework Boolean / JScript boolean
Number	.NET Framework Double / JScript number
String	.NET Framework String / JScript string
Int	.NET Framework Int32
Long	.NET Framework Int64
Float	.NET Framework Single
Double	.NET Framework Double
Object	.NET Framework Object / JScript Object
Date	JScript Date object
Array	JScript Array
Function	JScript Function object

The other major performance improvement added to JScript.NET is the introduction of Option Fast. This option tells the compiler to enforce certain rules that allow additionally optimizations, at the cost of some reduced functionality. When Option Fast is enabled, the following JScript behavior is activated:

- You must declare all variables.
- You cannot assign values to, or redefine, functions.
- You cannot assign to, or delete, predefined properties of the built-in JScript objects.
- You cannot add **expando** properties to the built-in objects.
- You must supply the correct number of arguments to function calls.
- The **arguments** property is not available within function calls.

The new Option Fast feature helps you write faster code, but it does change the behavior of the language—so just adding Option Fast to an existing JScript program may result in one or more compiler errors. Nevertheless, with some small changes to your program, you should see some significant performance improvements.

Compilation

One of the key new capabilities of Jscript.NET is the ability to compile to .NET IL (Intermediate Language), which means that, with some effort, JScript code will produce essentially the same compiled code as Visual Basic.NET, C#, or any other .NET language. Finally, script developers will be able to get those compiler nuts off their backs and get on with their work. (Scripters know that having to go through a compilation phase to get an EXE or a DLL is *so* 20th century, but we'll keep that under our hats for a while longer.)

Although compiling is a pain when you want to write a quick script, it does have its uses—and JScript.NET allows you to compile your script into an EXE or a DLL, so that you can send out precompiled code rather than having to compile source every time.

Productivity

Now that you've got your JScript code running much faster, hopefully you'll be compelled to write more JScript code, and, probably, larger programs. Writing larger programs in JScript today can be quite difficult, since it doesn't provide many mechanisms to encapsulate code—and the code you write isn't necessarily the most robust. JScript does have a prototype inheritance model that allows for encapsulation, but it's not very well known, and even less well understood. It's also a very "fragile" sort of encapsulation, making it difficult to write robust code. If you try to reference a property on the object that doesn't exist, JScript will simply add it for you, rather than telling you it's not there. This feature is commonly known as **expando** properties, and it makes picking up JScript very easy, since you can extend existing objects very easily. Expando functionality, however, is a dual-edged sword, since this flexibility ultimately makes it difficult to write robust, large-scale scripts.

To address this, JScript.NET introduces classes and packages to the language. Classes allow you to develop objects to encapsulate functionality and data very easily, with the added advantage of being able extend existing classes (single inheritance for your sanity, if nothing else) and implement interfaces. The best thing about this is that, because JScript is a fully-fledged .NET language, you can extend (or implement) any class (or interface) defined in any other .NET language—and vice-versa.

By default, classes in JScript don't support dynamic properties (expandos), thus allowing you to sidestep the issues they might cause. Nevertheless, in the spirit of evolving the language and allowing classes to be used with existing code (helpful if you're writing a class library), and because they're a cool feature, JScript classes can handle dynamic properties by marking the class as **expando**.

Declaring classes in JScript is achieved via the **class** statement, which contains methods and properties defined by using familiar **function** and **var** declarations. If you're familiar with the current JScript syntax for creating constructor functions, the migration to classes should be pretty simple for you. For most objects, you need only enclose the constructor function with a class of the same name, declare the class members, and move the function declarations inside the class. If you mark the enclosing class as **expando**, you don't even need to declare the class members, although your code won't be as robust. For example:

JScript 5.5 code

```
// Simple object with no methods
function Car(make, color, year)
{
    this.make = make;
    this.color = color;
    this.year = year;
}


function Car.prototype.GetDescription()
{
    return this.year + " " + this.color + " " + this.make;
}


// Create and use a new Car object
var myCar = new Car("Accord", "Maroon", 1984);
print(myCar.GetDescription());
```

JScript.NET code

```
// Wrap the function inside a class statement.
class Car
{
    // Declare the class members. I've used types in this example,
    // but they are not required. I could have also marked the class
    // as being 'expando' and not had to declare these members.
    var make : String;
    var color : String;
    var year : int;

    // Old constructor function, unchanged.
    function Car(make, color, year)
    {
        this.make = make;
        this.color = color;
        this.year = year;
    }
```

(continued)

(continued)

```
    // Move the function inside the class
    function GetDescription()
    {
        return this.year + " " + this.color + " " + this.make;
    }
}

// Create and use a new Car object
var myCar = new Car("Accord", "Maroon", 1984);
print(myCar.GetDescription());
```

By default, the **function** and **var** declarations within a class declare publicly visible functions and properties. JScript.NET also supports private and protected properties and functions; just add **private** or **protected** in front of the **function** or **var** declaration to get the desired visibility.

JScript.NET also supports the declaration of property accessors—custom functions that run when a property is read or written—by using the **get** or **set** modifiers. For example:

```
class Person
{
    // Private variables -- actual data can't be seen
    // outside the class
    private var m_sName : String;
    private var m_iAge : int;

    // Constructor -- called to create new objects
    function Person(name : String, age : int)
    {
        this.m_sName = name;
        this.m_iAge = age;
    }

    // Name is read-only as there is no 'set' function
    function get Name() : String
    {
        return this.m_sName;
    }

    // Age is read-write, but can only be set to
    // "meaningful" values
    function get Age() : int
    {
        return this.m_sAge;
    }
```

```
    function set Age(newAge : int)
    {
        if ((newAge >= 0) && (newAge <= 110))
            this.m_iAge = newAge;
        else
            throw newAge + " is not a realistic age!";
    }
}

var fred : Person = new Person("Fred", 25);
print(fred.Name);
print(fred.Age);

// This will cause a compiler error - Name is read-only
fred.Name = "Paul";

// This will work
fred.Age = 26;

// This will give a run-time error, as the value is too large
fred.Age = 200;
```

Inheritance

A JScript class can inherit and extend an existing class written in JScript or any other
.NET Framework language (e.g., C#, Visual Basic) by adding the **extends** keyword after
the class statement. This ability allows JScript programs to take advantage of the
richness of the .NET platform very easily. To illustrate this, I wrote a simple JScript
program that creates a Windows 2000 service (a frequent request from script authors).
The script consists of a class that extends the .NET Framework's **ServiceBase** class.

```
/*    Simple JScript service
      Andrew Clinick July 2000
*/

// Import the required .NET namespaces.
import System;
import System.ServiceProcess;
import System.Diagnostics;
import System.Timers;

class SimpleService extends ServiceBase
{
    private var timer : Timer;
```

(continued)

(continued)

```
// Constructor -- setup the service properties
function SimpleService()
{

   CanPauseAndContinue = true;
   ServiceName = "JScript Service";


   timer = new Timer();
   timer.Interval = 1000;
 . timer.AddOnTimer(OnTimer);
}

// Method called when the service starts
protected override function OnStart(args : String[])
{
   // Create an entry in the event log, and start the timer
   EventLog.WriteEntry("JScript Service started");
   timer.Enabled = true;
}

// Method called when the service stops
protected override function OnStop()
{
   EventLog.WriteEntry("JScript Service stopped");
   timer.Enabled = false;
}

// Method called when the service pauses
protected override function OnPause()
{
   EventLog.WriteEntry("JScript Service paused");
   timer.Enabled = false;
}

// Method called when the service continues
protected override function OnContinue()
{
   EventLog.WriteEntry("JScript Service continued");
   timer.Enabled = true;
}

// Method called every time the timer clicks
function OnTimer(source : Object, e : EventArgs)
```

```
    {
        EventLog.WriteEntry("Hello World from JScript!");
    }
}


// Create and run the service
ServiceBase.Run(new SimpleService());
```

The **SimpleService** class extends the **ServiceBase** class; it also has some functions that override the various event handlers in ServiceBase. When the class is loaded, it automatically gets all the functionality required to be an NT service—and the only real code I had to write was the script for hooking up to the Timer and writing out to the event log every second. Notice how by including the **System.Diagnostics** namespace, I can just call out to **EventLog.WriteEntry**; it does all the Windows API calls required to actually write the text to the event log.

I won't go into packages at length here, but they provide a mechanism to create a namespace into which classes can be added. This allows further flexibility in encapsulation, since you can put a set of like classes into a package—making it easier to package up code (pardon the pun).

Debugging

No matter how much better we make the JScript language, programmers will still make errors, and so great debugging support remains a key requirement for increasing developer productivity. We've enhanced the debugging capabilities in Jscript.NET to allow full Visual Studio.Net debugging. Those of you who have struggled with debugging JScript 5 will welcome the new debugging features, which are now built on the same technology that is used by Visual Basic.Net and C#. Suffice to say that you can step through code, set break points, use immediate and watch windows, and use other great debugging features in JScript just as you can in the other Visual Studio.Net languages.

Examples Using JScript.NET

The primary focus for this release of Jscript.NET is for scripting on the server—and, in particular, the new capabilities provided by ASP+. To illustrate using ASP+, I've written a few simple demos.

ASP+ page accessing SQL Server

The first demo is a simple ASP+ page using JScript.NET and the new data access classes in the .NET Framework. I've used the familiar <% %> scripting mechanism to query the authors table in the SQL Server pubs sample database. I know it isn't very exciting, but it illustrates some of the new features in JScript:

```
<%@ Import Namespace="System.Data" %>
<%@ Import Namespace="System.Data.SQL" %>
<%@ language="JScript" %>
<link rel="STYLESHEET" type="text/css" href="style.css">
<%
// Setup the connections, commands and datasets
var myConnection:SQLConnection = new
SQLConnection("server=scripting;uid=sa;pwd=;database=pubs");

// Execute the SQL
var myCommand:SQLDataSetCommand = new SQLDataSetCommand("select * from Authors",
myConnection);


// Set up my variables and type them using the new
// typing feature in JScript
var ds:DataSet = new DataSet();
var myTable:DataTable
var myColumns:ColumnsCollection
var myCol:DataColumn
var myRows:RowsCollection
var myRow:DataRow

// get the data by calling the FillDataSet method
myCommand.FillDataSet(ds, "Authors");
myTable = ds.Tables[0]
%>

<h1>
<%=ds.Tables[0].TableName%>
</h1>
<br>
<TABLE>
 <THEAD>
 <TR>
<%
//Iterate through the columns in the table and
// write out the column names at the top of the table
myColumns = myTable.Columns
for (myCol in myColumns)
{
%>
 <TH class="spec">
 <%=myCol.ColumnName%>
 </TH>
<%
```

```
}
%>
 </TR>
 </THEAD>
<%
// Get all the rows and write out a TR for each row
myRows = myTable.Rows
//Notice how I can now iterate through collections
//using for in rather than the enumerator object
for (myRow in myRows)
{
%>
 <TR>
<%
    for(var i:int=0;i<myColumns.Count;i++)
    {
%>
 <TD class="spec">
<%=myRow[i]%>
 </TD>
<%
    }
%>
 </TR>
<%
}
%>
</TABLE>
```

A key point in this script is the ability to iterate through collections using for ... in.
If you're a JScript developer today this is major step forward, because you no longer
have to worry about what type of collection you're working with; JScript just does the
right thing.

Another important note is that ASP+ provides is the ability to bind controls to datasets.
This means you wouldn't even have to write any of this script, but I thought I'd keep the
process familiar for this example.

Creating a Web service

In the past, the only way you could create a Web service using JScript was via Remote
Scripting. Remote Scripting is a great technology—but it's limited, because you can call
the service only from a browser, and the format of its XML messages is proprietary.
The onset of SOAP as a standard way to call Web services makes the proprietary format
of the XML even less palatable. Fortunately, ASP+ provides a great way to define Web
services.

All you need to do is create a JScript.NET class and put it into an ASMX file. ASP+ does the rest. ASP+ creates the Service Description Language (SDL) automatically, and handles any SOAP requests. I converted my Weather Web service to be fully buzz-word compliant in a couple of minutes. Here's the ASMX file:

```jscript
<%@ WebService Language="JScript" class="Weather"%>

import System
import System.Web.Services

class Weather {

   WebMethodAttribute function getConditions(strCity : String) : String
   {

   var now = new Date();
   switch (strCity.toUpperCase())
   {
        case "LONDON":
            if (now.getMonth() <= 7||now.getMonth() >=9)
            {
                return "overcast"
            }
            if
            {
                return "partly overcast"
            }
            break;
        case "SEATTLE":
            if (now.getMonth() == 7 && now.getDay()==4)
            {
                return "torrential rain"
            }
            else
            {
                return "rain"
            }
            break;
        case "LA":
            return "smoggy"
            break;
```

```
        case "PHOENIX":
            return "damn hot"
            break;
        default:
            return "partly cloudy with a chance of showers"
    }
  }
}
```

Summary

JScript.NET is a major evolution of JScript and the scripting platform, providing a rich, robust language that builds on the existing script language while providing a flexible way to start building bigger scripts. The key to all of these enhancements in JScript and Visual Basic is the .NET Framework on which they are built. The .NET Framework provides even more scriptable objects for you to use in your solutions, and extends the capabilities of your scripts to allow just about anything to be scripted on your machine or on the Internet. This is just the first stage of JScript.NET, and we'd love to get your feedback on how we're doing and what we can do in the future.

OWNER REGISTRATION CARD   *Register Today!*   0-7356-1446-6

Return the bottom portion of this card to register today.

Microsoft® Visual Studio.NET

FIRST NAME	MIDDLE INITIAL	LAST NAME

INSTITUTION OR COMPANY NAME

ADDRESS

CITY	STATE	ZIP

(   )

E-MAIL ADDRESS	PHONE NUMBER

U.S. and Canada addresses only. Fill in information above and mail postage-free.
Please mail only the bottom half of this page.

For information about Microsoft Press®
products, visit our Web site at
mspress.microsoft.com

Microsoft®